mosQues

mosQues

RAZIA GROVER

Lustre Press
Roli Books

ISBN: 81-7436-441-2

© **Roli & Janssen BV 2006**
Published in India by
Roli Books in arrangement with
Roli & Janssen BV
M-75, Greater Kailash-II Market
New Delhi 110 048, India.
Phone: ++91-11-29212271, 29212782
Fax: ++91-11-29217185
Email: roli@vsnl.com
Website: rolibooks.com

Editor: Amit Agarwal
Design: Inkspot
Layout: Naresh Mondal

Printed and bound at Singapore

Photo credits

Ajit Saran: 133, 134 (bottom).

Corbis: Front & back cover, 6-7, 12, 16-17, 18, 20, 21, 22, 24, 24-25, 26-27, 28-29, 30, 32-33, 34, 35, 36-37, 38, 39, 40, 42, 43, 44, 46-47, 48-49, 50, 51, 53, 54-55, 56, 57, 58, 61, 62, 63, 64, 65, 66, 66-67, 68, 69, 70-71, 72, 73, 74, 76-77, 79, 81, 82-83, 84, 85, 87 (bottom), 88, 89, 90, 91, 92-93, 94, 95, 96, 97, 98, 100, 101 (top, middle, bottom right), 102, 103, 105, 112, 114, 124-125, 129, 130 (top), 131, 132, 136, 140, 141, 142-143, 144.

Getty: 2-3, 8-9, 14-15, 17, 23, 47, 80.

Lucy Peck: 106-107, 108, 110, 116, 117, 118.

National Geographic: 86, 87 (top).

Roli Collection: 13, 101 (bottom left), 119, 121, 122-123, 126, 130 (bottom).

The Aga Khan Trust for Culture: 134, 135, 137, 138, 139.

Monica Gautam/ Vipul Garg (illustrations): 19, 31, 41, 45, 47, 52, 59, 65, 71, 75, 78, 108, 109, 111, 113, 115, 118.

Anis Khan (map): 10-11.

Preceding pages 2-3: The Haram Mosque in Mecca is considered by Muslims to be the holiest place
in the Islamic world, and is the focal point for their pilgrimage or Haj.

For Satish

"Only he shall inhabit God's sanctuaries who believes in God and
the Last Day, and performs the prayer, and pays the alms, and fears
none but God alone."   – Koran, Sura 9.18

"I do not want my house to be walled in on all sides and my
windows to be stuffed. I want the cultures of all lands to blow
about my house as freely as possible. But I refuse to be blown off
my feet by any one of them."   – Mahatma Gandhi

Author's Note

This book was to have been written by my architect husband Satish Grover. Already an author of four books
on Indian architectural history, this would have been his first attempt at writing on buildings outside India. On
his sudden passing away in 2005, Roli Books asked me to complete the book, barely begun. I am honoured by
their faith in my being able to accomplish the task. The book is basically in two parts, the first part featuring
the great historic mosques of the world. These are located chapter-wise according to their location and, by and
large, their chronological place in history. For this section I would particularly like to acknowledge the writings
of Henri Stierlin, Markus Hattstein, Sheila Blair and Jonathan Bloom. Though the basic selection of the
mosques for this part had been done by Satish, I have added to it. For the chapter on the Indian subcontinent,
I have been guided by Satish's book on Indian architecture. For the second part of the book, which is the
contemporary section, I have consulted the book by Renata Holod and Hasan-Uddin Khan, though the
selection is completely mine. I also thank Malini Saran for her input on Indonesia. I am grateful to the
publishers for giving me this opportunity to learn more about the history and architecture of these
timeless buildings.

Decorated vaulted ceiling, Friday Mosque, Isfahan.
Following pages 8-9: Istanbul's Suleimaniye Mosque located on the Golden Horn of Turkey.
The mosque announced the unequalled greatness of the Ottoman sultan, Suleiman the Magnificent.

C o n t e n t s

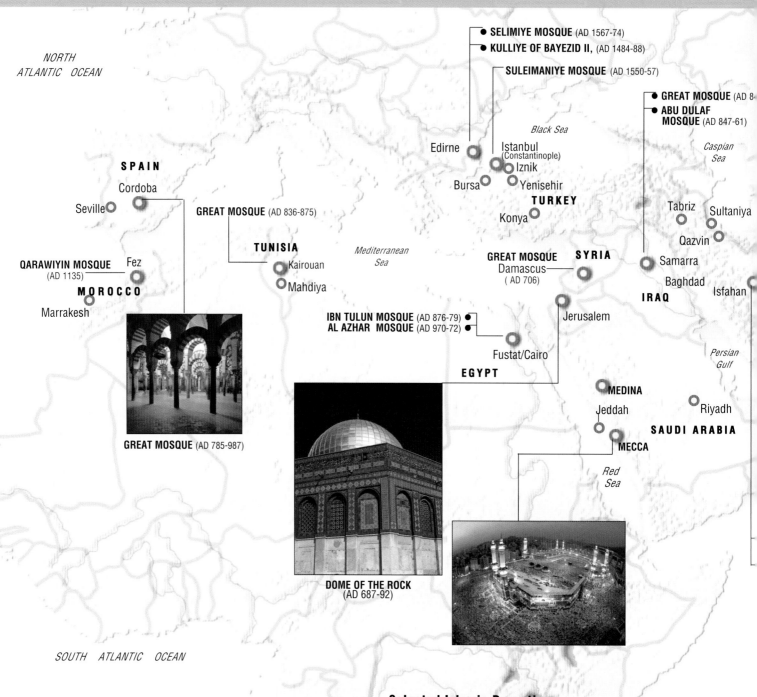

NORTH
ATLANTIC OCEAN

● **SELIMIYE MOSQUE** (AD 1567-74)
● **KULLIYE OF BAYEZID II,** (AD 1484-88)

SULEIMANIYE MOSQUE (AD 1550-57)

● **GREAT MOSQUE** (AD 8
● **ABU DULAF MOSQUE** (AD 847-61)

Black Sea

Caspian Sea

Edirne
Istanbul
(Constantinople)
Iznik
Bursa
Yenisehir

TURKEY

Konya

Tabriz   Sultaniya

Qazvin

Samarra

SPAIN

Cordoba

Seville

GREAT MOSQUE (AD 836-875)

Mediterranean Sea

GREAT MOSQUE
Damascus
(AD 706)

SYRIA

IRAQ

Baghdad   Isfahan

QARAWIYIN MOSQUE
(AD 1135)   Fez

MOROCCO

Marrakesh

TUNISIA

Kairouan

Mahdiya

Jerusalem

IBN TULUN MOSQUE (AD 876-79) ●
AL AZHAR MOSQUE (AD 970-72) ●

Fustat/Cairo

EGYPT

Persian Gulf

GREAT MOSQUE (AD 785-987)

● **MEDINA**
Jeddah

● Riyadh

SAUDI ARABIA

MECCA

Red Sea

DOME OF THE ROCK
(AD 687-92)

SOUTH ATLANTIC OCEAN

— ● Selected Islamic Dynasties ● —

● **Abbasids** AD 750-1258
Capital: **Baghdad** (main),
from AD 762;
Samarra AD 836-83/92
Overthrown by Mongols
AD 1258. Shadow caliphate
under Mamluks in
Cairo AD 1260-1517

● **Aghlabids** AD 800-909
Capital: **Kairouan** (main),
Overthrown by Fatimids

● **Almohads** AD 1130-1269
Capitals: **Marrakesh, Seville**
Overthrown by Merinids

● **Almoravids**
AD 1056/60-1147
Capital: **Fez** (main),

Marrakesh, from AD 1086;
Overthrown by Almohads

● **Anatolian Seljuks**
(Rum Seljuks) AD 1077-1308
Capital: **Iznik** (main),
Konya from AD 1116
In AD 1308 territory
becomes province of
Persian Ilkhanids

● **Ayyubids** (indep of
Ayyubids of Yemen)
AD 1171-1250/60
Capitals: **Damascus, Cairo**
subdivided from AD 1193;
Cairo branch ends AD 1250;
Damascus & Alleppo branch
ends AD 1260

● **Sultans of Delhi**
AD 1206-1526
Slave dynasty AD 1206-90;
Khaljis AD 1290-1320;
Tughlaqs AD 1320-1414;
Sayyids AD 1414-51;
Lodis AD 1451-1526/1540-56;
Suris AD 1540-55

● **Mughals**
AD 1526-40/1556-1857
Capital: **Agra** (main),
Last emperor deposed
by British

● **Fatimids** AD 909-1171
Capital: **Kairouan** (main),
Mahdiya; **Cairo** from AD 973

Overthrown by the Ayyubids

● **Ghaznavids** AD 977-1186
Capital: **Ghazna** (main),
Lahore from AD 1156

● **Ghurids** AD 1150-1206/12
Capital: **Firuzkuh** (main),
Lahore (in AD 1186)
Succeeded by Delhi Sultanate

● **Ilkhanids** AD 1252/56-1335
Capital: **Tabriz** (main),
Sultaniya from AD 1307.
Empire breaks up AD 1335

● **Indian Sultanates**
Adil Shahis,
Bijapur AD 1490-1686
Qutb Shahis,

MOSQUES OF THE WORLD

MONGOLIA

UZBEKISTAN

Bukhara

Samarkand

TURKMENISTAN

Merv Balkh

Herat Firuzkuh Kabul

IRAN AFGHANISTAN

Ghazna Islamabad

Yazd

Lahore

PAKISTAN Delhi

Agra

Fatehpur Sikri

Thatta

Jaunpur

Champaner

Arabian Sea

INDIA

Bidar

Golconda
Hyderabad

Gulbarga

Bijapur

CHINA

BIBI KHANUM MOSQUE (AD 1399-1494)

BADSHAHI MOSQUE (AD 1674)

● **QUWWAT UL-ISLAM MOSQUE** (AD 1193, 1230, 1315)
● **BEGUMPURI MOSQUE** (AD 1387)
● **JAMI MOSQUE** (AD 1644-58)

JAMI MOSQUE (AD 1572)

● **ATALA MOSQUE** (AD 1408)
● **JAMI MOSQUE** (AD 1458-79)

JAMI MOSQUE (AD 1523)

JAMI MOSQUE (AD 1367)

JAMI MOSQUE (AD 1570)

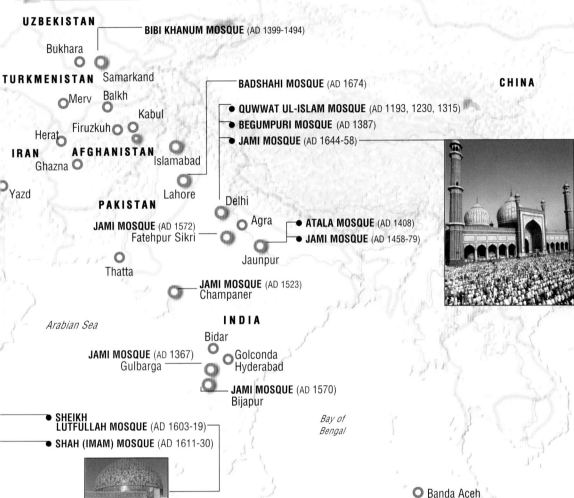

● SHEIKH
LUTFULLAH MOSQUE (AD 1603-19)

● SHAH (IMAM) MOSQUE (AD 1611-30)

Bay of
Bengal

Banda Aceh

INDIAN OCEAN

INDONESIA

Golconda AD 1512-1687
Barid Shahis,
Bidar AD 1487-1609
Bahmani Sultans,
Deccan AD 1347-1527
Malwa Sultans,
Malwa AD 1401-1531
Sharqi Sultans,
Jaunpur AD 1394-1479
Sultans of **Gujarat**,
AD 1396-1583

● **Islamic Mongols**
After Genghiz Khan's death
AD 1227, 4 sons become
founding fathers of Mongol
tribal organizations. Dynasty
ends with defeat of Golden
Horde branch by Timur

● **Mamluks** AD 1250-1517
Capital: **Cairo** (main)
Overthrown by Ottomans

● **Merinids** AD 1244-1467
Capital: **Fez** (main)
Overthrown by Wattasids

● **Ottomans**
AD 1280/1300-1922
Capitals: **Yenisehir** AD 1326;
Bursa AD 1326;
Edirne AD 1366;
Istanbul/Constantinople
from AD 1453
Caliphate disbanded AD 1924

● **Safavids** AD 1501-1722/36

Capital: **Tabriz** (main);
Qazvin AD 1548;
Isfahan from AD 1598
Shadow rulers in some
provinces AD 1722-36;
power transferred
finally to Qajars

● **Seljuks** (Great Seljuks)
AD 1038-1157/94
Capital: **Merv, Isfahan** (main)
Disintegration begins AD 1092

● **Spanish Umayyads**
AD 756-1031
Caliphs/emirs of
Cordoba AD 929;
rulers of **al-Andalus**

AD 756-1031
Split into states

● **Timurids** AD 1363/70-1506
Capital: **Samarkand** (main);
Herat from AD 1405
Overthrown by Shaybanids

● **Tulunids** AD 868-905
Capital: **Fustat** (main)
Reconquered by Baghdad
caliph AD 905

● **Umayyads** AD 661-750
Capital: **Damascus** (main)
Overthrown by Abbasids AD 750

CHAPTER 1

The Mosque in History

MECCA AND MEDINA

The great mosques of history were built across kingdoms covering most of the ancient civilizations, from the deserts of Arabia and North Africa to the vast expanses of West and Central Asia and India.

In more recent times, this universal symbol of Islam has added to the built environment of cities and towns in a contemporary idiom. While retaining the generic features of the Muslim congregational place of worship, the mosque today also exhibits the latest technological and material advances in architecture.

From the very first prayer hall – Prophet Muhammad's house in Medina, which was subsequently enlarged and restored and is accepted as the first masjid (place of prostration) in history – the story of mosques is also that of the histories of great empires. While mosque architecture was influenced by the Arabic tradition in Mesopotamia, Syria, Egypt, North Africa and Spain, it also evolved through three other major traditions – the Persian, Turkish and Indian.

MUHAMMAD, THE PROPHET OF ISLAM

Muhammad, the founder of Islam, was born in Mecca around AD 570 in a society of nomadic tribes, whose settlements shifted as swiftly as the dunes of the desert. A tough and hardy people, their axiom was 'survival of the fittest'. Inter-tribal looting and warfare was common. In their daily endeavours they sought the blessings of supernatural powers that were a strange mix of the pagan and early Jewish and Christian icons. Muhammad's tribesmen, the Quraish, were the guardians of a pagan shrine in Mecca, which housed a black cubic stone known as the Kaaba. Muslims

Prayer mat depicting the Haram in Mecca.
Facing page: Sunset prayers at Mecca just before the start of the Haj pilgrimage.

believe this to be the house that the prophet Abraham had built for God. They recognize Abraham as the first Muslim and the first prophet, and accept the teachings of both the Old Testament and the Torah.

As he witnessed the discord among Arab tribes, Muhammad began to preach the message of unity. Despite opposition to his ideas, he persevered and gradually began to forge an Arab identity. Muhammad must have had a premonition of his destiny, for in about the year AD 610, he heard the voice of God through the angel Gabriel, revealing to him the message of 'Islam' (submission to God). The message convinced him of the existence of only one God, Allah, challenging the prevalent pagan practices of worshipping many gods. The message also emphasized the equality of all men in God's eyes. Astonishingly, such a radical notion for those turbulent times began to find gradual acceptance. Soon Muhammad was recognized as God's messenger, the last prophet. The one who became a believer was called a Muslim (one who submits himself to God). The Koran (literally meaning recitation) is a record of the revelations of God to Muhammad, and it is precisely for this reason that the written word assumes such importance in Islamic art and culture, both as language and as a decorative medium.

Muhammad, along with his growing following, continued to be derided by many in Mecca, particularly within his own tribe and the rich merchant class, of whom he was one and who scorned the new creed. He was forced, along with his small band of followers, to flee Mecca for Medina, a nearby oasis, in AD 622. This journey, or the Hegira (emigration), marks the date from which Islam takes all its dates. Today, Mecca and Medina are the most sacred places in

The Kaaba, destination of Haj pilgrims, is a grey stone cubic building which only Muslims can enter.
It contains the sacred Black Stone which the angel Gabriel is believed to have brought to earth.

Ancient Arab practices ritualized the worship of idols and other magical icons, which Muhammed destroyed in AD 630,
leaving only the Kaaba, which pilgrims are required to circle seven times during the Haj pilgrimage.
Facing page: The ritual namaaz (prayer) is said five times a day.

the Islamic world. Millions of Muslims flock to these two cities not only to celebrate the birth of Muhammad, but also to make the pilgrimage, or Haj, at least once in a lifetime. The Haj is believed to guarantee the everlasting blessings of Allah. The Kaaba is the focus of the pilgrimage, which now lies at the centre of the Haram Mosque (a later construction) at Mecca, and from here, the ten-day-long ceremonies end in Arafat, about 20 kilometres east of the city.

The Haj is one of the five Pillars of Islam, the first four being the tenets: 'There is no God but Allah and Muhammad is his Prophet'; prayers five times a day, accompanied by prostrating oneself in the direction of Mecca and reciting certain verses according to a set ritual; fasting during the

To touch the holy Black Stone inside the Kaaba is the ultimate desire of every Muslim who goes on pilgrimage to Mecca.
Facing page: Reconstructed sketch and plan of the Prophet's house in Medina and the mosque built around it later by Caliph al-Walid.

month of Ramadan; and giving zakkat, or alms, to the poor, of a fixed percentage of one's income.

MEDINA, THE FIRST MASJID

Muhammad soon acquired the status of a religious and political head. He was both a pacifist and an astute strategist, who realized the need to consolidate and expand his spiritual following in order to strengthen and defend the faith. This was accomplished, more often than not, through war (jihad), considered acceptable in the name of God. In Medina, where he lived for about ten years, his house naturally became the centre of all religious and community activity. The domestic accommodation comprised no more than a few small rooms, built on one side of a partially enclosed square. Over a period of time, as the number of his followers grew, the courtyard became a convenient area in which to meet, pray and to listen to his teachings.

As temperatures were high in the region, the need for shelter from the scorching sun was soon met by the creation of a verandah in the northern front of the house. The wall of the verandah, facing Jerusalem at that time, became the qibla (direction for prayer). A second portico was added to the south side when Muhammad returned to Mecca from Medina after proclaiming the supremacy of the Kaaba over Jerusalem. A high chair or stool from where the Prophet addressed the faithful, next to the qibla, became the first minbar (pulpit, for sermons and announcements), an element that was given increasing importance in the design of the mosque as it evolved. The Prophet's house was enlarged after his death in AD 632.

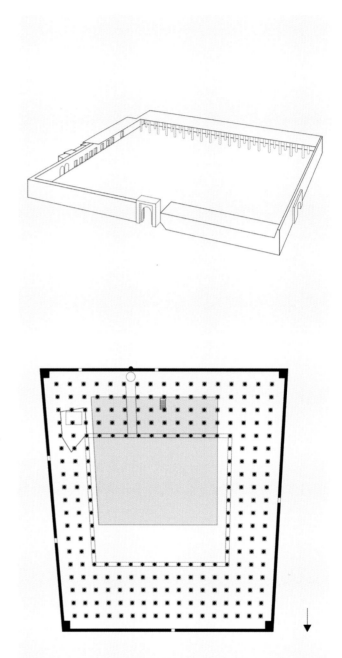

The vast courtyard of the Mecca mosque accommodates thousands who come together on festive occasions.
Facing page (top): Located near a port city on the Red Sea, Mecca was a meeting point for the caravan trade;
(bottom): The mihrab in the Prophet's House Mosque.

THE MOSQUE

To safeguard their sanctity, the great mosques were almost always surrounded by an enclosure. This not only ensured a physical withdrawal from the affairs of the world, but also a spiritual retreat, reinforced by the placing of the most sacred part of the mosque, the mihrab (arched niche), at the farthest and most secluded end from the entrance. Islam does not predicate the authority of an intermediary or a priest. The communion with God is very personal and therefore the namaz (ritual of prayer) can be conducted anywhere, not necessarily in a preordained place of worship, as long as one faces the general direction of Mecca. The faithful pray, wherever they may be, at any of the five specified times of prayer from dawn to dusk – it may be in a room, a garden or an open space, an office or even the street. Thus, a mosque could be a temporary structure, defined by a few stones, as it must have been in the early days when the crusading armies of Islam were embarked on jihad.

It is only on Fridays that Muslims come together for the noon prayer, when a sermon is delivered by the imam, or leader of the community (hence the term jami, meaning Friday, mosque). The imam is the custodian of the mosque, and therefore considered the highest spiritual authority in the mosque's jurisdiction. Before imams took over this role, the caliph or ruler was both the religious and political head.

Originating from the need for a place where the faithful could gather together to pray, the mosque was essentially a community space. It served a practical function where all kinds of day-to-day affairs were conducted. It was a basic rectangular or square space – decoration was definitely not a consideration in the earliest mosques. Size was, for the area

had to be large enough to accommodate the entire, and rapidly expanding, community. The mosque thus reinforced a sense of identity and cohesiveness.

It was the Friday mosque that received the major endowments and architectural attention, whether from the ruler, the state or private patrons. The language of the mosque, with all its symbolic elements, became clearer after the Prophet's death, and the variations in detail that are subsequently seen in the great mosques of the world, all owe their special qualities to regional influences, and the patronage of those who had them built. Representative of mosque architecture was the qibla; the mihrab; the minbar; the central water body for cleansing oneself before praying; the maqsura, or windowed enclosure, specially reserved for the ruler or important authority; smaller platforms for other notable persons; columned hall and surrounding galleries; and the minarets, proclaiming the mosque's location and used to call the faithful to prayer.

The minarets are said to be a derivation of the church towers. The single minaret originated in Mesopotamia and North Africa, in the early Seljuk period (eleventh century). In both Turkey and Persia, the double minarets appear at the courtyard entrance. In Turkey, a single minaret was often placed off the central axis, somewhere in the courtyard. Extravagant caliphs could build up to six minarets around the prayer hall. The Kaaba, in fact, has seven. The minaret was a structure used not only for mosques but for mausoleums too. The minarets could be tapering, tiered, fluted, cylindrical or capped, either by sharp conical forms, cupolas, or small pavilions. The minarets also provided a base for beautiful carving, calligraphy, tiling or other sculpted patterns.

The minbar, originally used to preach as well as dispense justice, is used today exclusively as a pulpit, and elaborately decorated.
Facing page: The decorative elements of Muslim architecture in Spain included horseshoe and multifoil arches, perforated screen partitions and elaborate tile work.

As the mosque assumed greater social, and even political, significance in its role as a symbol of a ruler or patron's power and also his artistic sensibilities, it became more aesthetically pleasing. The iwans (vaulted halls around the courtyard), for instance, were typical of the style developed in Iran post-eleventh century. These were painted and sculpted in intricate detail, creating an appropriate sense of awe and wonder upon entering the house of prayer.

The dome was never an obligatory element in a mosque but it was developed to emphasize the central area of worship in it. The dome inspired great heights of engineering brilliance, particularly by the Ottomans, who installed this feature with an unequalled flamboyance. Indian rulers also paid great attention to the domes and semi-domes in their mosques, an outstanding example of symmetry and elegance being the mausoleum of the Jami Mosque in Delhi.

THE SPREAD OF ISLAM

Before his death in AD 632, Muhammad had returned to Mecca to win over his enemies, and through his astute diplomatic skills he succeeded in doing so. To appease them, he accepted the sanctity of the Kaaba, although he destroyed all other idols in the temple, and thus established the pivotal place of the Black Stone at the heart of the most sacred of Muslim shrines. The message of Islam soon spread rapidly through conquests. Omar, the second caliph, or successor of the Prophet, gave the movement its first major thrust. He was brilliant both in war and statesmanship, and gave the Islamic empire a solid organization. Within two years (AD 635-37), Damascus, Jerusalem and the whole of Syria and Palestine had fallen to the crusading armies of Muhammad's

successors, the caliphs. The Sassanian Persians lost Iraq and Iran in AD 637, along with Ctesiphon, near present-day Baghdad. This was accomplished by Sa'ad ibn al-Waqqas, a favourite follower of the Prophet. The remains of a mosque built in nearby Kufa, and burnt by Caliph Omar out of jealousy, still exist, bearing all the fundamental characteristics of a courtyard, a prayer hall and probably a domed chamber.

By AD 640 the Muslim armies had marched westward into Egypt and soon after, annexed the North African province of Ifriqiya (present-day Tunisia), and the Maghreb, on the coastal belt of Algeria and Morocco. In AD 711 most

Calligraphy on tile mosaics, and *(right)* carved stonework and floral arabesques at the shrine of Imam Reza in Mashad, Iran.

24

Pilgrims walk between Safa and Marwah, two stations of pilgrimage within the Great Mosque at Mecca.
Following pages 28 & 29: Tile work outlines architectural elements covering the surface
in the upper part of the Dome of the Rock façade.

of Spain, except for parts of the north, was conquered. Iraq and south Persia also succumbed to the advancing caliphs. But by now infighting had begun among the Arab leaders, which included members of Muhammad's family (Ali, his cousin and fourth caliph) and other followers (Muawiya, Ali's secretary and governor of Syria). Eventually, after the assassination of Ali, Muawiya was elected caliph in AD 660. Islam went through its first division. Those who believed that Ali was the legitimate caliph or imam were henceforth called Shias, while the majority described themselves as Sunnis (from sunna, meaning 'custom', referring to the rules of conduct set by the Prophet).

Muawiya was the founder of the Umayyad dynasty. Medina, the original capital of the expanding caliphate, now lost its status to Damascus, the capital of Syria, which already had a fine tradition of building art. By the end of the seventh century, Muslim troops spread eastwards from Iraq into Central Asia, Afghanistan, modern Pakistan and India, opening the way for this part of the world to come under the spell of the young religion. It was only after a semblance of internal peace had been achieved under the caliph Abd al-Malik in AD 692, that the Umayyads turned their focus to more creative pursuits.

The greatest of Abd al-Malik's architectural successes were in Jerusalem (Dome of the Rock) and Damascus (Great Mosque). He was also the first to enlarge Muhammad's house in Medina and give it the formal status of a mosque. It was during his time that a mihrab was first added to the Prophet's House Mosque. One of the reasons ascribed to its inclusion is that Coptic Egyptian workmen were employed in the renovation. They were used to building apses on the side walls of churches, and decided to make one here too.

CHAPTER 2

Jerusalem

DOME OF THE ROCK

Jerusalem occupied a singularly important role for believers of the new faith because it was this city that the Prophet first directed his followers to face while praying. Jerusalem was the site of the first Temple of Solomon, and the place of Adam's burial. It was from here that Muhammad was supposed to have made his miraculous night journey to heaven, and here that Abraham prepared to conduct the sacrifice of his son Isaac. All of these sacred spots are contained in a complex known as the Haram al-Sharif. It was only later, after his revelations, that Muhammad changed the focus of prayer to the Kaaba in Mecca. An unusual inscription inside the Dome of the Rock glorifies Islam and makes mention of the prophets and Jesus and Mary, but the real intention of this was probably to place Islam as superior to Christianity and to draw unbelievers to the true faith. Nevertheless, the Dome of the Rock was venerated by Muslims, Christians and Jews alike.

The city of Jerusalem is surrounded by hills sheltering a maze of congested houses, alleys and winding bazaars. Walls protect and divide the people, splitting the city into separate communities. A nervous tension runs through the daily life of its inhabitants, strangely bound together by the weight of religious and political history that the city is seeped in. Emblematic of their common past is the glowing cupola of the Dome of the Rock that rises above the western wall.

The Dome of the Rock was built by Abd al-Malik between AD 687 and 692, presumably to surpass the pre-eminence of the Kaaba, which was in the hands of a rival caliph (scholars challenge this as a later ninth-century interpretation). It is situated at the centre of a rocky outcrop, Mount Moriah, also known as Temple Mount, where a British pilgrim, Bishop

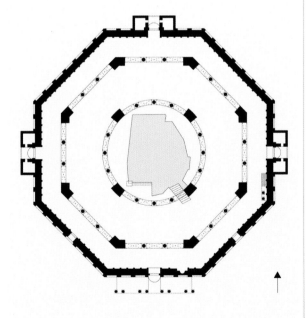

Plan of the Dome of the Rock. *Facing page:* The exterior of the Dome of the Rock adorned with tile work, an Ottoman addition to the building.
Following pages 32 & 33: Rising magnificently above the city of Jerusalem, the gilded dome shelters the stone where Abraham prepared to sacrifice his son and from which Muhammad took flight on his night journey.

Arculf, reported seeing an earlier mosque in AD 670. Nearby stands the Church of the Sepulchre, built by Constantine over Christ's burial place in Golgotha. This earlier Byzantine building, as well as the Church of the Ascension at the Mount of Olives, appear to have been the inspiration for the Dome of the Rock. In any event, the entire Temple Mount was cleared and rebuilt by the caliph. Although not strictly a mosque, the Dome is supported by spatial and other elements that suggest mosque typology and place it at the beginning of a long chronology of mosque architecture. For this reason it is also one of the three pillars of the sacred architecture of Islam, the other two being the sanctuaries of Mecca and Medina.

It was natural that these early buildings of Islam should inherit the tradition of Byzantine and Christian architecture. Like the great basilicas of Christianity, the Dome of the Rock is a sumptuous work of art. Octagonal in plan, the enclosure encompasses the central bare rock surface over which the dome soars 118 feet (36 metres) high, supported on a cylindrical drum. The four cardinal points have arched entrances with porches, the south facing and largest one being prominently fronted by four pairs of columns. Inside, alternating pillars and Corinthian columns form two concentric circumambulatory paths around the sacred rock.

Although the seventh-century building retains its original form, it has gone through some changes. The present cover of gilded copper on the dome, for instance, is a twelfth-century replacement of the original in lead. Restoration work has been carried out several times since. The dome itself is made of two wooden shells in the Syrian tradition of using this lightweight material to span large spaces. The tiles above the

window line were installed by the Turks in AD 1554 to replace the original glass mosaic.

Koranic inscriptions form an intricate border on the exterior and interior wall surface. However, unlike Byzantine decoration, which included figures and scenes from the Old and New Testaments, the imagery here is of plants and flowers, and of regal and religious symbols. Awesome in its magnificence, only the Dome's small mihrab, simply panelled with black and white stone, is a reminder of the original, mystical intent of the shrine. Scholars have suggested a cosmic patterning of the geometric layout, with the octagonal, square and circular spatial concepts merging in perfect unison, "symbols of the ideal, unchanging and perfect world of the hereafter." (Henri Stierlin, art historian.)

Calligraphic inscriptions form part of the glittering interior of the Dome of the Rock, giving information about its renovation in the twelfth and fourteenth centuries. *Facing page:* Restored in 1818, the Dome of the Rock's interior is painted, gilded and inscribed in concentric circles.

AL AQSA MOSQUE

The second most important building in the Haram al-Sharif is the mosque known as Al Aqsa, built by Abd al-Malik's son al-Walid between AD 707-709. It replaced the earlier 'mosque' described by British pilgrim Bishop Arculf. There have been so many reconstructions of this building since then that its original form remains unknown. An earthquake in AD 747 caused it extensive damage and thirty years later, it was rebuilt by Caliph al-Mahdi.

In the Haram al-Sharif, the mosque was built specifically for the purpose of congregational prayer, although the entire area of the Temple Mount is considered so holy that a pilgrim can pray anywhere he likes. After Mecca and Medina, the Al Aqsa is the holiest of Muslim mosques and despite the political tension that has prevailed in the city in recent times, it is still the most visited of the three as non-Muslim visitors are also allowed here, unlike in the other two.

The mosque is on the north-south axis to the Dome of the Rock, and directly orientated towards Mecca. The only part of it that remains true to its original form is the point where the corridor leads to the mihrab bay and is surmounted by a cupola, originally made of wood. It appears to have had seven naves in all, perpendicular to the qibla and separated by arcades, and eleven bays. The central bay was wider and higher, as in the Cordoba mosque built seventy years earlier. The minbar, destroyed in the twentieth century, was one of the most outstanding examples of the Aleppo woodcarvers' craft. Parts of the interior still show signs of the original mosaic work on a gold background.

Rebuilt several times, the Al Aqsa Mosque in the Haram al-Sharif is surrounded by a warren of crowded settlements and ruins.

CHAPTER 3

Damascus

GREAT MOSQUE OF DAMASCUS

The ancient city of Damascus has been described as the Garden of Paradise, and its Great Mosque a foretaste of heaven itself. The city's cool streams, verdant pastures and gardens are likened to a green brocade gown by the traveller Ibn Jubayr, who visited it at the end of the twelfth century. Inside the Great Mosque, built by the prolific builder Caliph al-Walid, existing panels of mosaic testify to an idyllic landscape of tall trees with dense foliage and gurgling streams, bordered by lavishly decorated mansions, dream palaces and pavilions.

The Great Mosque itself was a dazzling work of architecture, both in appearance and design. Its longitudinal layout has been likened by Henri Stierlin to the desert where Arab horsemen "rode side by side in a single row across a wide expanse while across the more fertile lands criss-crossed by roads, groups and bands travelled single file." The imagery is evocative of the congregational mass of praying men in the mosque, immersed in individual supplication but powerfully united as their voices echo through the vast columned and open spaces of the mosque to invoke the blessings of the One and Only God.

Mosques of the Umayyad period followed the model of the Prophet's house in Medina. They normally made use of existing garrison structures in towns that had been newly set up during the military advances of the Muslim armies. The courtyard grew in size as the numbers of followers increased, eventually becoming almost four times the size of the Medina house.

After he enlarged the Prophet's house in Medina into a mosque and built the Al Aqsa Mosque, al-Walid turned his attention to Damascus. Here, in the elevated centre of the city, on the site of an ancient temenos, he

An exquisite mosaic detail. *Facing page:* In the corner of the courtyard of the Great Mosque of Damascus is the Treasury Chamber, a small octagon covered with mosaics.

Aerial view of the Great Mosque of Damascus, constructed in AD 705 under Caliph al-Walid.
Facing page: Reconstructed drawing of the Great Mosque, built on the ancient sacred
site (shaded) where the basilica of St John the Baptist must have stood.

started the construction of a mosque. The Temple of Jupiter had stood here in the first century AD and, at the end of the fourth century, after Christianity arrived, the Byzantines had converted it into a great basilica dedicated to John the Baptist. Later, the Muslims used a part of the church for their congregational prayers until their numbers increased to require a larger building, which the caliph then built (AD 704–714). Although the basilica was demolished to give place to the new mosque, a small shrine stands integrated with the mosque in honour of John the Baptist.

Caliph al-Walid demolished the church but retained the large 525 x 328 feet (160 x 100 metre) fortress-like enclosure. Instead of the original west-east axis of the church, he changed the orientation of the prayer hall to the south, directly facing Mecca. For the first time, the prayer hall was set in a niche and 'walled' with columns and arches, highlighting the sanctity of this space in the mosque hierarchy. This feature set a precedent for later mosques. The temenos was converted to an oblong courtyard surrounded by porticoes on three sides. The prayer hall side was built up with three longitudinal bays, the centre of which was surmounted by a cupola. This space was made into a maqsura for the caliph and the imam. The dome emphasized the sovereign status of the ruler.

Large arcades and at least forty Corinthian columns, 19.6 feet (six metres) high, along with smaller arcades and columns, suggest the Byzantine style, proving that these elements were reused from the buildings that preceded the mosque on the temenos. A two-storeyed passageway runs around three sides of the courtyard. Al-Walid refashioned the square towers at the two southern corners of the mosque into minarets, while a new one was built at the north gate or Gate of Paradise.

The profusion of landscape detail in various parts of the

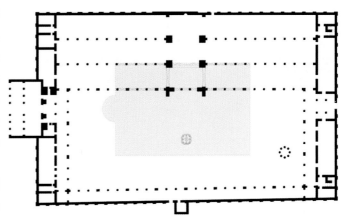

mosque is also typical of the Byzantines. This is apparent over the main entrance to the prayer hall, as well as on the small octagonal treasury chamber resting on marble columns at the western corner of the courtyard. Elsewhere, geometric stone patterns on the window grills and mosaics on some of the columns are early examples of the non-figurative Islamic decoration that was to become a hallmark of Muslim art. According to some, the mosaic surface area in the Damascus mosque was probably the largest in the world, covering a vast space of 43,000 square feet (4,000 square metres).

The caliph requested the Byzantium emperor to send him Greek labourers, "for I mean to build a mosque the like of which my predecessors never constructed, nor will my successors ever raise such a building." According to Ibn Batuta, the Persian historian, he employed twelve thousand artists from Constantinople, among them mosaicists, whose exceptional artistic imagination and handiwork adorned the walls of the mosque. Unfortunately, a massive fire in 1893 destroyed much of this. A large part of the prayer hall was subsequently rebuilt. The cupola, mihrab and minbar were among the areas that were reconstructed. Islamic calligraphy

and fine geometric patterning depict the early development of this style of decoration.

The Umayyads remained powerful for about ninety years, when rivalries began to break the eastern part of their territory. Unable to keep control over rival factions, the last Umayyad caliph shifted his capital to Haran, close to northeast Iran, but he soon had to flee to Egypt, where eventually he and all his family, but one, were murdered. The surviving member took refuge as far west as he could on the shores of North Africa, from where he entered Spain to found the emirate of Cordoba, the first region to break free of the control of the traditional Islamic leadership.

Although the Umayyads created many exceptional buildings, their architecture and art did not have strong distinguishing characteristics. During the first century of Islam, builders had to resort to reusing materials from earlier Roman temples and Christian churches, and their artisans were used to the Hellenistic or Byzantine idiom. In Cairo, Damascus, Kairouan, Cordoba, wherever hypostyle halls had been the style, it was easier to convert these into mosques, rather than create entirely new structures. Nevertheless, there is more than a hint every so often of a new sensitivity that eventually flowered into the Persian or more eastern heritage. By the end of the twelfth century, there were about 250 mosques and over twenty madrassas in Damascus.

The Umayyad caliphs were eclectic but hedonistic. It was only with their successors, the Abbasids, that the Islamic arts found a mature identity, as Baghdad became the hub of a religious, scientific and artistic flowering. Religion was now codified, and diplomacy, economy, trade and literature flourished. Persian influences soon began to displace those from the Mediterranean.

One of the few existing mosaics in the Damascus mosque projects a stylized vision of the legendary city, believed to have sheltered the Messiah and his mother. *Facing page:* Public and private buildings in Damascus made extensive use of ancient tall Corinthian columns.

CHAPTER 4

North Africa and Andalusia

GREAT MOSQUE OF CORDOBA

The early plundering forays of the warriors of Islam into the rich Iberian peninsula turned into a more permanent occupation after AD 711. The Visigoth kingdom of Spain was at the time ruled from the royal centre of Toledo. A rival Christian faction in Toledo, rebelling against the tyranny of the monarch, soon threw the Visigoth nation into civil war. The leader of the rival faction sought the help of the Arabs and their allies across the Strait of Gibraltar. The ruler of Tangiers, Tariq, offered to do so, and rallying the Berber Muslim troops, crossed over the Strait. He finally entered Toledo victorious in AD 712. Within two years, the Muslims had occupied all of Spain, which they called Al-Andalus. Christian Spain had been crushed and even the future French emperor, Charlemagne, was held at bay at the borders. For the next eight hundred years, Spain was dominated by Muslim rule.

Cordoba was one of the cities where the Muslims settled down. Here, they initially used a church to pray, sharing it with the Christian community. It was only when Abd al-Rahman became emir in AD 756 that Cordoba was made a capital city and the mosque of Cordoba was built to announce the supremacy of Islam in Spain. Work on the Great Mosque of Cordoba began in AD 785. (The final phase of additions ended in AD 988, two hundred years later.) It was a classic example of the hypostyle hall segmented into several bays with interspersed columns and arches. Again, like the buildings following the Christian or Roman heritage, many of the columns, pillars and capitals were reused elements. The roof was of timber.

Built near the Guadalquivir River, on the site of the demolished San Vincente church, the mosque was initially a 230-feet (70-metre) square

Interlaced arches of the maqsura in the Great Mosque, Cordoba. *Facing page:* A forest of columns and arches with alternating light and dark stones in the prayer hall of the Cordoba mosque forms one of the most electrifying spaces in mosque architecture.

The interior of the dome of the Cordoba Mosque, covered with mosaics in the rich Byzantine style.
Facing page (top): Stages of Cordoba Mosque's enlargement; *(bottom):* Another view of
the interlaced arches of the Cordoba Mosque.

building and consisted of an oblong hall, which was preceded by a courtyard that was more wide than long. The structure was enlarged four times, first under Abd al-Rahman II in AD 832-48. Eighty years later it underwent its second transformation. A third and almost final enlargement took place between AD 961-76 under al-Hakam, who transformed the prayer hall from an oblong area to one that was still 230 feet (70 metres) wide but whose length was now increased to 377 feet (115 metres). From the original ten marble columns, the hall roof was now supported by 320. Finally, in AD 987, al-Mansur widened the sahn (courtyard) extensively and added eight aisles to the east.

Through its four successive enlargements, the mosque acquired an enormous plan and some spectacular imagery. And despite a sixteenth-century addition, after the Reconquista, when a Renaissance cathedral was added rather incongruously to the mosque's central area after demolishing sixty-three pillars, it remains one of the classics of Islamic architecture. Each change was handled with such finesse that though visibly apparent, it retained a remarkable unity of style with the existing structure.

The building covered 3.7 acres and in its final form the prayer hall had nineteen naves running perpendicular to the qibla. The hall was divided by a veritable forest of columns and horseshoe arches. The courtyard became almost the same size as the prayer hall, probably to accommodate the vast population of the city. The double-tiered columns were spanned by horseshoe arches, banded in stone and brick, soaring upwards towards the wooden ceiling and accentuating the central aisle.

Among the most spectacular parts of the mosque are the maqsura and the mihrab. Richly decorated, the maqsura has

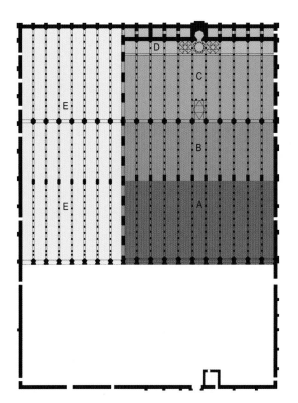

a sense of screened enclosure, imparting a special effect to the sacred centre. The mihrab itself is not a simple recess, but a small octagonal enclosure of multifoil arches that one enters through a horseshoe arch embellished with sumptuous gold-and-polychrome mosaics. A small cupola covers it. Above all this rises the main dome, splendidly decorated with mosaic work on a gold background.

Next to the mosque, Abd al-Rahman made his residence on the site of an existing Visigothic palace. This closeness of the religious and secular centres facilitated movement between the two. Of the four gates, only the western one, called the Minster's Gate, still exists in its original form. There was also no minaret when the mosque was first built and the palace tower was used to call the faithful to prayer.

There is nothing to equal the magic of the prayer hall of Cordoba anywhere else in the world. It is immense yet contained, exuberant yet solemn, its dark and light materials tantalizingly bewitching in the play of light that transforms the multitude of simple structural elements into a vibrant space. It has been described by the political historian Tariq Ali as having been created "by architects who understood the city and had participated in the intellectual ferment that thrived within its walls. There is something magical about this mosque... its refusal to be enclosed... all paths lead to emptiness... in this specially created void only the Word exists, but in Cordoba the mosque was constructed as a political and public space, not simply for the word of God." Even Charles I of Spain, responsible for the cathedral addition and heavy baroque imagery at a later date, is said to have admonished his builders with the words: "You have built what can be seen anywhere and destroyed what is unique."

The Great Mosque of Kairouan, seen here from its tall minaret, set the style for subsequent mosque buildings in the Maghreb and North Africa. Here, for the first time, glazed tiles were used.

GREAT MOSQUE OF KAIROUAN

The Great Mosque of Kairouan was built in the province of Ifriqiya (modern Tunisia), which the Arabs annexed in AD 670, at which time they founded the city of Kairouan. The fugitive Umayyad caliph had commanded a following here after his break with Baghdad. However, he was soon driven out and a governor was appointed in his place by the Abbasids in Baghdad. This was the military general Ibrahim ibn al-Aghlab. Ifriqiya was made a hereditary emirate on condition of paying tax to the Abbasids.

The first in a line of eleven emirs of the Aghlabid dynasty, Ibrahim ibn al-Aghlab made Kairouan his capital in AD 671, a city inhabited by Berbers, Romans and Africans. The Berbers followed a more orthodox interpretation of the faith and refused to be dictated to by the ruling class and the Arabs. Local Berbers were in constant conflict with one another. Despite the unrest, Kairouan became a centre of religious debate, and trade and building arts and

Top and right: The Berbers from the Sahara built mosques that were both fortified and finely and colourfully decorated.
Facing page: The oblong prayer hall of the Great Mosque of Kairouan had seventeen naves
made of reused antique and Byzantine columns running perpendicular to the qibla.

crafts flourished – encouraged by the proximity of the ruins of a classical ancient city nearby.

Ibrahim ibn al-Aghlab's successor, Ziyadatallah I, rebuilt the Kairouan Great Mosque after destroying the original, simple sun-dried brick construct that had stood there since the founding of the city. Following its first rebuilding in AD 836, the Kairouan mosque underwent two more reconstructions in AD 862 and AD 875.

The mosque, otherwise conforming to the standard plan set by its predecessors, especially of the Abbasid style of a courtyard surrounded by arcades, with a hypostyle prayer hall roughly one-third the size of the entire enclosed complex, has one outstanding feature – its minaret. Similar in form to the Lighthouse of Alexandria and other watchtowers of the region, it set a direction for the congregational mosques that were subsequently built in North Africa. The minaret looms over the wall opposite the mihrab, not exactly in line with the central aisle. It towers in a slightly slanting rectangular form in three layers of receding width, linked by an internal stairway. Capping the uppermost pavilion is a fluted cupola.

Kairouan, considered the fourth most important holy city of Sunni Islam, was destroyed in AD 1057. The eleventh century witnessed great turmoil as tribes directed by the Fatimids of Cairo rampaged across the Maghreb, North Africa and Andalusia. Small factional Muslim principalities emerged. Christians and Muslims fought each other or, against common rivals, even alongside each other. This unrest came to an end with the entry of the Almoravids, or warring Bedouins, whose mission was to fight for the faith.

Originating from central Sahara, the Almoravids were a confederacy of Berber tribes. Their leader was a Malikite legal professor, Ali ibn Yasin, who had been invited from Kairouan by a chieftain of one of the tribes to teach theology to his people. Ali ibn Yasin established a monastery (ribat) specifically to train religious warriors. The name Almoravid derives from al-murabitun (men of the ribat). They lived by the rules of the fatwas (Islamic legal opinions) and vehemently rejected any figurative representation of the Divine in Islamic art and life.

In AD 1061, Yasin's successor, Yusuf ibn Tashfin (AD 1061-1106), founded the capital Marrakesh, after having brought

One of the most beautiful spaces in the architecture of the Almoravids is in the Qarawiyin Mosque in Fez, which has three exquisitely tiled ablution pools in its courtyard. *Facing page:* The minaret of the Great Mosque of Kairouan.

The courtyard of the Qarawiyin Mosque, the largest of its time in the Maghreb, is enclosed by rows of sloping green tiled roofs built over different periods.

the whole of present-day Morocco under his control. Conquering Fez in AD 1069, his march of victory took the Almoravids as far east on the Mediterranean coast as Algiers. They were ascetic to the extreme and had no architectural tradition of their own. By AD 1094 the whole of the south of Spain was ruled by them and, in another fifteen years, the entire Muslim region of Al-Andalus and much of the northern part of the interior of Africa up to Sudan. Their contact with Spain influenced a style widely termed as Hispanic-Moorish today.

In AD 1098 Yusuf ibn Tashfin assumed the title of Amir al-muslimin (Ruler of the Muslims), following the Baghdad precedent, where the caliph was called Amir al-muminin (Ruler of the Believers).

QARAWIYIN MOSQUE, FEZ

The Qarawiyin Mosque is named after Kairouan, having been built by the people who came from that city in the ninth century. By the time its last rebuilding took place in AD 1135 (there were two intermediary stages in AD 912 and AD 933), its surface area covered 39,000 square feet (3,668 square metres), making it the largest mosque of its time in the Maghreb. There were five muqarnas (decorated vaults) along its raised central longitudinal axis, and as they caught the light, they created a kind of mystical pathway to the mihrab. An oblong courtyard with three ablution pools sits at the western end, ensconced by multiple bays at least three times its size. Based on its position and size it is felt that the courtyard itself must have been intended as part of the main haram or sacred centre of the mosque. This was a common feature in the Moorish style of mosques.

A special feature of mosques of this North African belt is the minbar, that was normally commissioned by the caliphs. These are masterpieces of woodcarving and marquetry and many were executed by the skilled woodcarvers of Cordoba.

On the Spanish mainland, in the meantime, there was constant conflict between the Muslims and the Christians. The latter's cause was further strengthened by the Crusades. Under threat from the north and subsequently also from the Almohads further south of Morocco, the Almoravid empire broke up, losing Marrakesh in AD 1147. Islam was given a new dogmatic thrust by the victorious Almohad dynasty.

The ideology of the Almohads was dictated by the doctrine espoused by a theologian and preacher, Ibn Tumart

(AD 1080-1130). He vehemently opposed the literal translation of the concept of God as a hearing and seeing entity, which imparted to Him a human quality open to polytheistic interpretation. He advocated instead the indivisible, metaphysical Oneness of God. His followers became known as al-muwahhidun (Confessors of the Unity of God) from which term the name Almohad is derived. Faced by militant opposition from the Almoravids, he retreated to the Atlas mountains to protect himself and his community. There he organized his followers, giving himself the title of the Mahdi (The Expected One) and even claiming to be descended from the Prophet. This effectively challenged the authority of the caliphs of Baghdad. After his death his mountain retreat was converted into a mosque in his memory.

FRIDAY MOSQUE OF TINMAL

The Friday Mosque of Tinmal is typical of the fortified cities and mosques of the Almohads. Their rigid doctrine is reflected in their architecture, particularly in mosques in which any deviation was akin to blasphemy. The mosque, built to honour Ibn Tumart, lies 100 kilometres southeast of Marrakesh, dramatically sited against the rugged mountains. Extensively restored, the building shows the existence of a surrounding wall with three entrances, a single minaret, a four-bayed arched gallery facing the mihrab, a wider central aisle forming a T with the transept, and elegant muqarnas (vaults) in front of the mihrab as well as at the outer corner of the transept. The plan of the brick building is square and the building itself is outstanding for its simplicity and purity of imagery.

The minbars of the North African belt were masterpieces of marquetry.
Facing page: Tinmal, the starting point of the Almohad movement, had a small mosque with a multiple-aisled and arched prayer hall running parallel to the qibla wall.

CHAPTER 5

Mesopotamia

BAGHDAD AND SAMARRA

The Abbasids derived their name from Abbas, an uncle of the Prophet. Under Abu al-Abbas as-Saffah, his descendant, the Islamic world was split irrevocably into different power centers: Cordoba, where the secessionist branch prospered till the beginning of the first millennium, and the eastern region of Iraq, where the Abbasid dynasty ruled for five centuries from AD 749 to 1258. The third was the province of Ifriqiya in North Africa.

Iraq was a coveted land made wealthy by the fertile soil of the Tigris and Euphrates rivers. It has been suggested that the fervour of the Arab believer was motivated not simply by religious zeal and the promise of Paradise, but by economic considerations as well. The Tigris and Euphrates not only offered the spoils of the land but also enviable trade routes to the Gulf and the Mediterranean. Iraq, in the golden age of Islamic civilization, became a crossroads of economic activity and with the convoys of valuable goods – precious stones, furs, silks and ceramics – from lands as far as China, came the merchants of knowledge – writers, historians, travellers and artisans. Mud deposits from the rivers provided abundant material for building and the technique of making sunbaked bricks ensured a permanence of structure.

The eighth and ninth centuries were a period of cultural flowering in Iraq. Baghdad was looked upon as a great centre of theology, law, history and architecture. The Arabic language had spread far and wide and given expression to sophisticated works of poetry and prose. Caliph Harun al-Rashid wrote the classic *A Thousand and One Nights* and Caliph al-Mamun established in AD 833 the Bait al-Hikma or House of Science. This was also a period when the Abbasid caliphs officially adopted the Shia persuasion, appointing the eighth imam as the political successor to the caliph al-Mamun. The Abbasids had been earlier supported by the Shiites from east

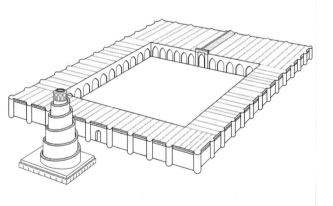

Called the Malwiya (snail-shell), the minaret of the Samarra mosque derives from Babylonian ziggurats.
Facing page: Spiralling monumentally upwards, the minaret of Samarra's
Great Mosque is a masterpiece of brick building technology.

Iran, at the time of their break with the Umayyads. They now inducted members of the Persian elite into their government while employing Turkish troops to guard their palaces.

After they had distanced themselves from the Umayyads and moved away from Damascus, the Abbasids set up their capital in the region around Kufa before moving to Baghdad. Baghdad was built on a circular plan, much like earlier Persian cities, by the caliph Al-Mansur in AD 762. The 'City of Peace' was located near the ancient cities of Ctesiphon and Babylon. Within its defensive walls there were government offices, houses, markets, and a mosque and a palace, both at the heart of three concentric rings of wall. The caliph enjoyed absolute power – both secular and religious. But because of the layout of the city's principal buildings, the privacy of the palace and the caliph's movements were greatly disturbed. Under the influence of the court style of the Persians, the rulers became increasingly conscious of their superior status, and withdrew to their palaces to conduct the social and political affairs of state. The mosque slowly began to lose its function as a people's forum for discussion and decision on matters concerning their daily lives, and became a place of purely religious activity. The preacher took the place vacated by the caliph and the sacred status of the mosque was reinforced.

The ulema or priestly class thus became a legitimate institution. The clergy took on the role of interpreting theological constructs of both the Koran and the hadith (the words and deeds ascribed to the Prophet). The caliphs, once regarded as Muhammad's spiritual heirs, were now reduced to political entities, who had to govern according to the Koranic interpretations of the ulema.

The influx of Turkish slaves, employed as soldiers for the caliphs, created a climate of dissent and rebellion. There was much unrest and an uneasy atmosphere prevailed, forcing the caliph to leave the city in the hands of Turkish chiefs in AD 836 and move to Samarra, a few miles north. Nothing remains on ground of the first city of Baghdad. When it later returned to being the capital of the Muslim world in AD 892, Baghdad was rebuilt on the eastern bank of the Tigris.

Caliph al-Mansur founded another city, al-Rafiqa, on the model of Baghdad in northern Syria, on the east bank of the River Euphrates. Here, the ruins of the Great Mosque show evidence of massive mud brick walls, strengthened by an upper layer of baked brick. The mosques of the Abbasid period conformed to a standard plan of a courtyard, surrounded on three sides by verandahs, a deep hypostyle hall roofed by wood, and the mihrab and minbar.

GREAT MOSQUE OF SAMARRA

In Samarra, Harun al-Rashid had already begun to build a palace before he moved his capital there. However, it was his grandson, the caliph Al Mutawakkil, who far surpassed the founder of the city in his building enterprises. The relics of two congregational mosques constructed by him are among the few remaining examples of buildings that can be seen in Samarra. Although they are in ruins today, there is still enough visual evidence that sets them apart from other mosques of the period. First, they were built of burnt brick, a material involving different methods of construction compared to stone mosques further west. In terms of scale, perhaps it was the openness of the country, after the confines of Baghdad, that offered the ruling class the freedom to build expansively. The Caliph al-Mutawwakil Mosque of 784 x 512 feet (240 x 156 metres) was by far the largest mosque in the world for

centuries. It was two-and-a-half times the size of the Great Mosque of Damascus. The mosque was isolated from the city by a ziyada (a surrounding enclosure encircling the courtyard walls). A fortress-like wall with forty-four buttresses and fourteen gates contained the main complex, covering ten acres. The entire site of the mosque covered about fifty acres.

The outstanding feature was the spiral minaret. This powerful form has been called the Malwiya (meaning snail shell) because of its likeness to that form. Having a height of 180 feet (55 metres), it was originally linked to the mosque by a bridge as it lay outside the main enclosure. It tapered upwards with an ascending ramp, culminating in a cylindrical pavilion, with columned arches moulded into it. More than a place to call the faithful to pray, the minaret proclaimed the presence of the mosque, perhaps thought necessary in the early crusading days of the new religion. It was as much a symbol of the faith as of the status of the person who built it.

ABU DULAF MOSQUE

A second mosque close to Samarra, in a place sometimes referred to as the Abu Dulaf district of Samarra, was also built by al-Mutawwakil in AD 847-61 to serve the people of that area. It is not as large as the first, but its remains reveal dimensions of considerable size – 699 x 443 feet (213 x 135 metres). Though it copied the essential features of the earlier mosque, brick arcades now spanned across square brick piers instead of across columns. The dimensions of the piers were so heavy that there was an overbearing sense of weightiness in the prayer hall.

In the second half of Abbasid rule, Baghdad came into the hands of first the Buyids (AD 945-1055), then the Seljuks (AD 1055-1194) and finally the Mongols, who effectively destroyed the city and the Sunni caliphate in the eleventh century. With them the dynasty effectively came to an end, even though under the Mamluks of Egypt (AD 1250-1577) they were nominally recognized. Baghdad further declined when it lost its importance as a crossroads of trade, with the discovery of the sea route between Europe and India. The city's chequered history includes rule by the Safavid Shahs of Iran and eventually by the great Ottoman sultans. The arrival of the British in the eighteenth century restored its importance and wealth as steamship travel on the Tigris was resumed and a process of modernization started.

Fortress-like walls of the Great Mosque of Samarra enclose the largest prayer area of the ancient Islamic world.

CHAPTER 6

Egypt

The first Egyptian mosque was built by the Arabs in the old garrison town of Fustat. It was named after the victorious general Amr ibn al-As, who founded it. Work on the Amr Mosque began in AD 642, a year after the Arabs arrived in Fustat, and over almost two hundred years, the mosque was renovated, rebuilt and enlarged several times.

It was typical of the style of the earliest mosques with the hypostyle form of construction, reusing old Roman columns and capitals, tying them together with wooden rods and arching them with stonework. A rectangular courtyard led to the consecrated prayer area.

Two hundred years after the original Amr Mosque was begun, the first Egyptian mosque of any significance was built – the Great Mosque of Ibn Tulun.

After the last of the Umayyads had fled Baghdad for Egypt and North Africa, Egypt and Baghdad effectively became independent provinces ruled by governors appointed by the Abbasid caliph in Bahdad. Ahmed ibn Tulun, the son of a Turkish slave, who rose to the rank of a general, was appointed governor of Egypt. The Great Mosque, built by him between AD 876-79, established his authority and that of the growing might and following of Islam.

IBN TULUN MOSQUE

Ibn Tulun had spent his early years in Samarra, where brick was commonly used. In Egypt, though the tradition of stone buildings had achieved breathtaking proportions, he reverted to the material of the country of his birth. With brick he created a structure which, at 459 x 380 feet (140 x 116 metres), was larger than any mosque built in Egypt. It had a spiralling

The muezzin calls. *Facing page.* Ibn Tulun's Mosque in Fustat was made in brick though the spiral minaret was later rebuilt in stone. Like the Great Mosque of Samarra, this mosque had an outer enclosure (ziyada).

Egypt's oldest mosque, Amr, plays host to a crowd of worshippers during Ramadan. It was started in AD 642 and after several renovations attained its final form in AD 827. *Facing page:* Plan of Ibn Tulun Mosque; and minaret of Amr Mosque.

minaret unlike any seen in Egypt – which Ibn Tulun copied from the Great Mosque of Samarra.

The mosque's plan is basic – there is a qibla, a covered prayer hall, columned and arcaded porticoes, and an open courtyard with a central fountain. However, the purely functional attributes of the building are transformed by certain features that lift its severity. For instance, the ziyada or exterior courtyard, while being a clever buffer against the crowded neighbourhood, extends the scale of the building. The courtyard fountain was built in AD 1269 by the Mamluks (they were originally slaves of non-Arab origin who were promoted as officers in charge of military duties by the Ayyubid dynasty). It is a small, covered, stepped and domed structure, a monument in miniature set off by the horizontal canvas of the arcaded courtyard. A tiny cupola surmounts the mihrab, prominent enough against the bare flat roof to indicate the pre-eminence of the most sacred part of the

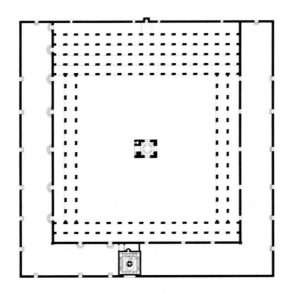

mosque. Slightly off the central axis, the spiral tapering minaret, again a later reconstruction in stone of an earlier brick structure, is eye-catching in its unfamiliarity. Situated at the eastern side of the site, in the ziyada, the original three-balconied minaret tower ends in an elegant third balcony, dome and finial, resting on a delicate base of slender look-through columns.

Finally, there is the stucco work lining the borders of arches, large and small, with intervening rosettes embedded into the wall spaces. The simple motif is repeated as a decorative border all along the top of the inner courtyard. Crowning the tops of the courtyard walls, an open work balustrade lends a lace-like embellishment to an otherwise sober, large building.

A muezzin at the top of a minaret calls the faithful to prayer from the Ibn Tulun Mosque, Fustat. The minaret, along with the dome, were later fifteenth-century Mamluk additions. *Facing page:* Gateway at the Ibn Tulun Mosque.

A fountain in the centre of the Ibn Tulun Mosque courtyard is unusually covered with a dome. *Facing page:* Views of the Al Azhar Mosque. A delicate railing on the roof and relief work on its walls decorate the courtyard enclosure.

Polychrome marble, almost mystical in its purity of design, highlights the mihrab, which is encased in stucco and stone. On one side, the wooden minbar displays more intricate geometric carving and tracery.

The Tulunid dynasty was succeeded by the Fatimids, who ruled Egypt for the next two hundred years (AD 909-1171). They were a Shiite Ismaili sect, whose leader, Ubaidullah, had proclaimed himself the Mahdi (The Expected One) and founded the Fatimid caliphate in Tunisia. However, he and his successors were unable to win over the local Berber and Sunni populace. From their base in Ifriquiya they had their eye on Egypt, the conquest of which was entrusted to a Slav officer, Jauhar. In AD 969 Jauhar mounted a successful campaign, conquered Fustat, and the Fatimids went on to rule Egypt in a spirit of relative tolerance towards the various religious communities that had settled there. This liberal outlook contributed greatly to building up a healthy economic climate and the creation of a new city – al-Qahira (Cairo), next to Fustat. In AD 973 Cairo became the capital of Egypt.

Fatimid fortunes were not destined to last long, however. They were opposed by neighbouring Sunni centres of power in the Maghreb and North Africa, and lost Syria and Palestine, which they had briefly occupied. Under Saladin, a powerful general in the service of the Syrians, the Fatimid caliphate was devastated and Abbasid supremacy restored over Egypt in AD 1171.

AL AZHAR MOSQUE

In the tradition of establishing a centre of worship after conquering a new city, the Fatimid rulers started work on the Al Azhar (meaning The Splendid) Mosque (AD 970–72). The building had several additions made to it subsequently. It was a focal point for theological debate in the Near East and one of the most important Shiite universities. After the fall of the Fatimids, it became a centre of learning of Sunni doctrine.

Not much remains of the original structure of the mosque but the additions are equally significant. Old columns and shafts were used in the building to support the arcades in stuccoed brick. The Mamluks added a domed porch to the mosque's original rectangular plan – with five aisles running parallel to the qibla.

Unusually slender columns form parallel bays to the qibla wall of the Al Azhar Mosque, whose plan is shown on the facing page.

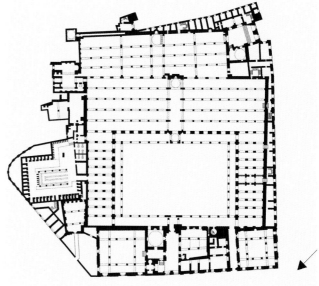

Cairo was really a palace city where the caliph and nobility lived. Few other mosques were built. The large al-Hakim Mosque built outside the city walls (AD 990-1012) was modelled after the Al Azhar Mosque but did not carry the same attraction, either architecturally or as a religious centre. Two others, the Aqmar and al-Salih mosques, built later, are much more refined, especially in the use of decorative elements. One feature common to most Fatimid buildings in Cairo was the attention given to stucco and stone ornamentation on both the exterior and interior of buildings.

Cairo developed as a vibrant city under the Mamluks in the thirteenth century. Even at this time, more mausoleums came up than mosques as each emir sought to perpetuate his memory, though there was a mosque at the centre of each complex. By this time, the Seljuk Turks had become a formidable power, bringing back Sunnism to erstwhile Shiite Egypt.

CHAPTER 7

Turkey

The Turks were robust nomads originating from the steppes of Central Asia. They spread westwards across the Oxus region to eventually command the largest enduring Islamic empire under the great Ottomans. By the tenth century, under the leader Seljuk, they had embraced Sunni Islam. By the eleventh century, various groups of the Seljuks commanded different territories. The most powerful, under Tughril Beg, moved westwards into Iran.

Driven by his own successes Tughril Beg set himself up as the protector of Baghdad's caliph, even claiming his daughter's hand in marriage in AD 1062. After Tughril Beg's death his nephew Alp Arslan (AD 1063-72), along with his vizier, Nizam ul-Mulk, established a consolidated Seljuk state, extending as far as Mecca. Under Malik Shah, Alp Arslan's son, the empire stretched from the borders of China to Anatolia in the west and Arabia in the south. After his death, rival Turkish tribes and self-seeking individuals in Anatolia and other regions tried to establish independent rule from time to time.

With true novitiate zeal the Turks set about the propagation of their newfound faith through building activity in the form of madrassas and mosques, besides constructing palaces, hamams and caravanserais. First under the Seljuks and later under the great Ottoman rulers, there was a flowering of all forms of architecture. The most important mosques, including the architectural masterpieces of the genius architect Koca Sinan (AD 1490-1588), were built between the fourteenth and sixteenth centuries. Many of the congregational mosques of these periods were surrounded by subsidiary structures such as the sahn, madrassa, hamam or tomb.

The Ottomans belonged to the group of Turkish tribes that had entered Anatolia and advanced towards Byzantium. Originally a pastoral

An Istanbul shoe-shiner. *Facing page:* Suleimaniye Mosque. From its warmer birthplace in Mecca, the mosque reached the colder region of Turkey, which demanded more enclosed spaces. These were domed in the typical Ottoman style, with many smaller domes becoming subservient to the main central one.

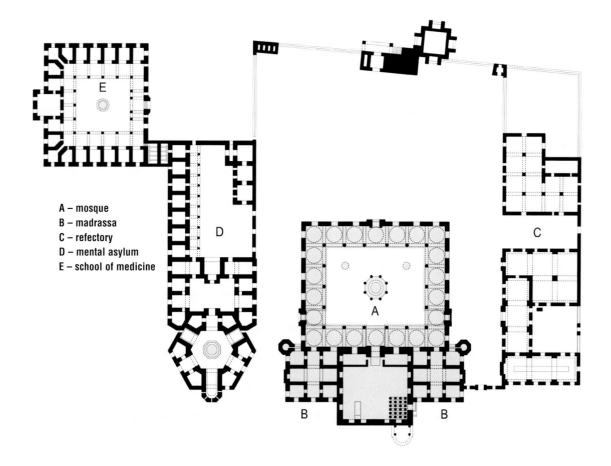

A – mosque
B – madrassa
C – refectory
D – mental asylum
E – school of medicine

people accustomed to living in temporary structures, they soon learnt the sophisticated techniques of building and decoration from the Persians, Syrians, Arabs and Armenians – all of whom they encountered during the course of their migratory forays.

With the capture of Constantinople (AD 1453), churches began to be converted to mosques. The cruciform plan of the Christian house of worship offered more longitudinal spaces, which could be spatially divided. The dome and semi-dome was extensively introduced. The most spectacular example of a church transformed into a mosque was that of the sixth-century Hagia Sophia, whose architectural features continued to be a major source of inspiration for the Ottomans. Sinan

referred back to this model repeatedly for his large repertoire of works. Sinan also drew inspiration from the buildings of his predecessor Heyruddin, another successful Turkish architect, whose scheme for the mosque complex, or kulliye, for Sultan Bayezid II at Edirne is described by some as the first masterpiece of Ottoman art.

MOSQUE COMPLEX FOR BAYEZID II, EDIRNE

Successor to Mehmet II, under whom Constantinople finally fell to the Ottomans, Sultan Bayezid II built the charitable complex (kulliye) around the mosque at Edirne.

Kulliye (welfare complex) of Bayezid II. *Facing page:* The mental asylum's domes and form echo those of the other buildings in the kulliye. *Following pages 76 & 77:* The Suleimaniye Mosque, built on a terraced site, encompassed a congregational mosque, six madrassas, two mausoleums, a Koran school and several charitable institutions.

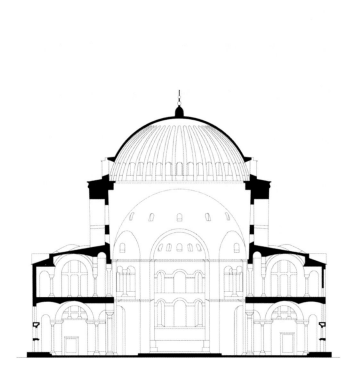

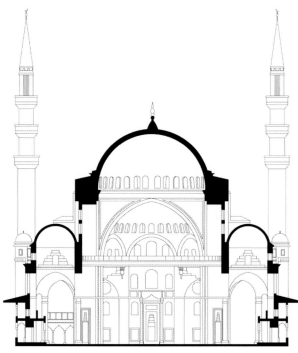

Vertically, the mosque is defined by two large minarets on either side, their width contrasting with the slender columns that support the arcaded corridor around the courtyard. Small, flattened domes all around the courtyard also accentuate the main dome over the square prayer hall. Heyruddin's signature element of a column placed on an axis is seen across the courtyard of the mosque, as well as in the school of medicine that is part of the kulliye.

Built between AD 1484-88, the kulliye is a skilful juxtaposition of opposing elements. While the cuboid higher mass of the mosque is in contrast to the horizontal 279 feet (85 metres) long spread of the hospital and mental asylum, there are two tall minarets looming over the lesser internal columns and external chimneys and small domes are pitted against larger ones. Walls are punctured by latticed small windows, arched above but rectangular at lower level. Twenty windows around the mosque's dome (having a diameter of 75 feet [23 metres]) illuminate a sober interior. Twelve small domes surround the main central one. Dressed stone on the wall surfaces is subtly enlivened by coloured ones, particularly to accentuate the arches.

Several influences can be seen in the evolution of the Turkish mosque, mainly from the Persians and, later, from the Byzantines. The Seljuks learnt the art of using the arch from the Persians, who had perfected the technique in brick. The arch was later used to imitate the vaulted spaces of Roman and Byzantine architecture. The dome was another influence – the earliest Turkish mosques (thirteenth and fourteenth

centuries) had simple domed rooms, often with colonnaded side aisles. Pendentives were freely used, but this element came more directly from both Armenian and Byzantine influence. Stone was the preferred material for Turkish buildings.

The dome was a special feature of Turkish architecture. Not for nothing has Istanbul been called the City of Domes. The skyline of many Turkish cities is studded with this solid form that swells and fades into the surrounding urban landscape. The best examples of Turkish architecture, however, do not convey a sense of excessiveness or superfluity. Instead, they offer a balanced composition between their various parts. And though they maintain a plainness in exterior surface treatment, they make up for it by the dramatic siting

of mosques (and other important buildings), always with a commanding view of the city as, for instance, on an elevated area or a visually striking point along a river.

Another peculiarly Turkish element is the minaret with a conical roof. This contrasted with its Persian ancestor of slender cylindrical towers capped by cupolas. Also, apart from surmounting the minaret with the conical roof, usually of wood, there were often two or more galleries along the length of the minaret tower.

The capital of the Seljuks was in Konya. When the dynasty faded away at the end of the thirteenth century, the new Ottoman rulers made Bursa, then Edirne, their capitals before settling on Istanbul (Constantinople).

The Turkish minaret had a typical needle point capping the top and two or three balconies breaking the length of the tower at regular intervals. *Facing page:* Sections of the Haghia Sophia *(left)* and Suleimaniye Mosque *(right)* show the influence of the former on the latter sultanic mosque.

THE SULEIMANIYE MOSQUE, ISTANBUL

The golden age of the Ottomans was heralded by Selim I, whose continued conquests brought international recognition to the empire. Preoccupied with his expansionist policies he, however, had little time for more artistic pursuits and it was left to his son, Suleiman the Magnificent, to glorify the successes of his father with more tangible signs of their power. The architectural flowering of Suleiman's reign must be attributed to the greatest Turkish architect of all time, Sinan. Though Greek (or Armenian) in origin, he served in an elite

corps of the Sultan's administration. In recognition of his extraordinary engineering abilities, he was appointed court architect in AD 1539, at the age of fifty. Over 350 buildings, both religious and secular, were designed and built by him. Among these are over eighty mosques and fifty prayer halls. The Sehzade Mosque was his first big success. It was commissioned by Suleiman in honour of his son, Prince Ahmet, who died as a young man (Sehzade in Turkish meaning 'crown prince'). The Selimiye Mosque at Edirne, another mark of his genius, was built in honour of Suleiman's successor, Selim II.

However, it was the Suleimaniye Mosque complex that surpassed all the mosques that Sinan ever planned or built. It announced the unequalled greatness of the sultan, who now ruled over a global empire. The sultan personally selected a prominent site on a slope above the Golden Horn, and work was begun on a date declared auspicious by an astrologer.

The prototype for the Suleimaniye is the Byzantine basilica, the Hagia Sophia, later converted to a mosque. This model, in turn, had symbolic reference to the original Temple of Solomon and through this association, the Sultan had deftly established both his legitimate imperial and divine lineage as well as the continuity of architectural tradition.

The Hagia Sophia had served as a prototype for several mosques, but using its basic formulation, Sinan added his own masterful perspective to make a bolder composition. Both have a basic octagonal plan, consisting of the main hall with a central dome, buttressed by semi-domes and a courtyard. However, though vastly diminished in size to the sixth-century basilica, the sixteenth-century Suleimaniye makes a more articulate statement. The domes and roof structure are clearer, revealing each component in its entirety. Inside,

Needle minarets and tiered domes of the Suleimaniye Mosque dominate the view from the Bosphorus. *Facing page:* Interior of Hagia Sophia.
Following pages 82 & 83: When the great Byzantine capital of Constantinople was conquered by the Ottomans,
the basilica of Hagia Sophia was transformed into a mosque.

instead of the arcaded galleries on either side of the Hagia Sophia's longitudinal axis, Sinan made wider arches to support the side domes. The courtyard too has domes on all four sides (the courtyard of the Hagia Sophia no longer exists).

So magnificent a work was it and so loved by the Turks that the Suleimaniye Mosque and complex became a symbol of Istanbul, and replicas of it would be sold and given away as gifts at important festivals.

Sinan was a master in planning. He had developed not only a successful basic blueprint for the design of mosques but also laid down visionary spatial concepts for the planning of educational and social buildings. This is why so many of his principal works are not just single-function buildings, but are complexes with several other uses.

The Blue Mosque in Istanbul is another gem of Turkish architecture. Though not designed by Sinan, it follows the master's example of perfect, and, in this case, a fairytale siting as it overlooks the Sea of Marmara and beckons one to the land of domes, minarets, mosques, madrassas, and other splendid works of architecture. Built between AD 1609-17, the Blue Mosque takes its name from the extensive use of brilliantly coloured tiles.

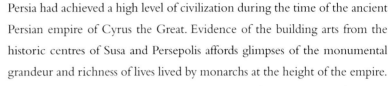

CHAPTER 8

Persia

Persia had achieved a high level of civilization during the time of the ancient Persian empire of Cyrus the Great. Evidence of the building arts from the historic centres of Susa and Persepolis affords glimpses of the monumental grandeur and richness of lives lived by monarchs at the height of the empire.

Before Islam came to Persia, the Zoroastrian faith was widely followed, in which fire, as one of the principal natural elements, was worshipped. The Zoroastrian fire temple, which consisted of a square building with four wide arched openings and a high dome, was the precursor of the first Persian mosques.

Persia had been under the domination of the Turkish Seljuks since the early eleventh century. The Turks provided the backbone of the military intelligentsia, while the more erudite Persians provided the bureaucracy. Isfahan was the capital of the vast Seljuk empire, where the first mosque built by them is one of the landmarks of religious architecture in Iran.

MASJID E-JAMI (FRIDAY MOSQUE), ISFAHAN

The Friday congregational mosque was built by Nizam al-Mulk, a Persian chief minister to the Turkish sultan Malik Shah, at the end of the eleventh century. Making use of an existing hypostyle building (dating to AD 840), Malik Shah demolished several of its columns in front of the mihrab. In their place he erected a freestanding domed chamber (or maqsura) for the sultan, supported on massive piers – thereby weakening the original structure. He had perhaps been impressed by the great dome of the Mosque of Damascus whose restoration work he had authorized. A second domed chamber was added by a rival of Nizam al-Mulk at the opposite, north end of the mosque. Undoubtedly elegant, it served no particular function but made for a near-

*Tilework in Sheikh Lutfullah Mosque, Isfahan. **Facing page:** The Masjid e-Jami (Friday Mosque) of Isfahan has the classic Iranian arched portal and minarets rising like horns.*

perfect vertical alignment of all the parts of the mosque, directing the eye in a smooth sweep to the decorated dome.

This influence of the Damascus mosque also points to the free flow of ideas and concepts across borders at that time. Travellers, historians and merchants all carried stories and picturesque accounts of the places they had visited, and though the details were not technically transferable, visually and conceptually the wonders of architecture – as also of other disciplines – captured the imagination of enlightened rulers and creative builders and craftsmen. Only the materials used in building and decoration changed according to their availability.

The Masjid e-Jami is reputed to have the largest courtyard in Iran (213 x 249 feet [65 x 76 metres]), in the centre of which is a pool made of marble. Various rulers added to the mosque, especially repeating the Persian element of the chehel-sotuni (forty-columned hall), so that the existing plan no longer remains a straightforward rectangle but has a rather amorphous footprint.

The most distinctive feature to be introduced by the Persians was the iwan. It was typically a high arched portal in the centre of each of the four sides of the courtyard. The largest and most imposing was the one at the entrance, visible to all, believers and non-believers alike, from outside. The shallowest

Aerial view of Shah Mosque, the more monumental of the two mosques abutting Isfahan's famous Maidan.
Facing page: (top) Courtyard of Shah Mosque; *(bottom)* decorative detail from Masjid e-Jami.

was at the entrance leading to the imposing, domed prayer hall. The iwan changed the entire imagery of the mosque. The character of the courtyard was dramatically transformed from an expansive, monotonous, usually open-to-sky space, to an awesome enclosure, calling attention to the splendid decoration endowed on the portals, and instilling an appropriate feeling of reverence when entering the confines of the hallowed space.

Seljuk rule was fragmented by the incursions of Mongols in the Oxus region and the Ghurids in Herat. The Mongol invasion of Iran devastated all that came in its path and construction activity all but stopped during this period. The mosques that remain display standard features of the Iranian

Tile decoration at balcony level of the Masjid e-Jami. *Facing page: (top)* Elaborate arabesque mosaic work and carved
stonework at the shrine of Imam Reza, in Mashad; *(bottom)* the northwest iwan of the Masjid e-Jami.

style, with a large courtyard and iwans and a domed prayer hall facing Mecca. The dome chamber was square, giving rise to an octagon supporting a sixteen-sided intermediary zone and the hemispherical dome. Sometimes the entrance portal was of a monumental scale, far exceeding in height the rest of the building.

The fourteenth century was marked by the military campaigns of Timur. He adopted the title of sultan and was responsible for forging a cultural unity between Iran and the Mongols. His empire extended from Aleppo in Syria to the borders of Hindustan. It included the entire region of Persia, from the Aral Sea to the Persian Gulf. The modern era in Persia begins with the coming to power of the Safavids in AD 1501, when Persian mosque architecture reached its zenith.

The Safavids were a Turkoman dynasty, originating from Azerbaijan on the Caspian Sea. Under their leader Ismail, they established their rule in Tabriz and within 150 years, ruled over a vast territory. They were Shias and having driven out the Sunnis, legitimized both a monarchic and theocratic state. Of the two main arms of the polity they naturally favoured their own Persian administrative elite, thus invoking the hostility of the Turkish military wing, with whom they maintained a delicate balance of power.

Under Shah Tamasp (AD 1524-76), they forged a national identity for themselves, but it was his grandson, Shah Abbas, who raised the nation to a high point of governance and culture. The empire was expanded to reclaim Iraq and other lost territories and now extended right up to the borders of Bukhara and Samarkand, coming down to the Persian Gulf past Mashad and Herat. Isfahan was made the capital in AD 1598.

Shah Abbas was an enlightened and liberal ruler, who patronized craftsmen and the arts, freeing them from religious

inhibitions. He cemented trade and diplomatic relations with other great empires such as those of the Czars and Mughals. By the time of his death, he had set Iran firmly on the forward path to modernization. It was during his splendid rule that the saying "Isfahan nisf-I jahan" (Isfahan is half the world) became popular.

It was under a later ruler, Abbas II, that the role of the shah became subservient to the religious orthodoxy. The weakness of his inept successors further strengthened the Shiite clergy, creating a climate of religious intolerance and loosening the hold of the Safavid dynasty, which effectively ended in AD 1726. Ten years later, Nadir Shah, one of the greatest conquerors in history, established his rule with Mashad as his capital. It was from here that he embarked on his devastating forays into Afghanistan and India, capturing the magnificent Peacock Throne from the court of the Mughal emperor Shah Jahan and rampaging through Bukhara and Khiva.

SHEIKH LUTFULLAH MOSQUE

When Isfahan was restored as the new capital by the Safavid Shah Abbas, the Maidan or large public square was the focus of all important buildings. It was located near the old congregational (Jami) mosque of the Seljuks. The Maidan, called Naqsh e-Jahan, was also symbolic of Iran's self-appointed status at the centre of the world. Spreading over an area of eight hectares, the rectangular space was flanked by baths, a mint, caravanserais, and a bazaar with jewellers, artisans, silk cloth merchants and dealers of exotic goods. Its coffee houses drew scholars and intellectuals, and ceremonial events and prestigious tournaments, patronized by the Shah, took place here.

An exuberance of decoration in the entrance portal of the Sheikh Lutfullah Mosque. *Facing page:* The domed room of the Sheikh Lutfullah Mosque is brilliantly covered with coloured tiles in a spiral arabesque design. *Following pages 92 & 93:* Isfahan's new Maidan is a vibrant place with the Sheikh Lutfullah Mosque on its east and the Shah Mosque on its south side.

Outside its enclosure, to the east, was the small but charming Lutfullah Mosque, named after a scholar and teacher. Only a small inscription over the doorway identifies this as a mosque and doubts remain about its exact function, although the essential elements of a mosque are evident. The qibla is set at a 45-degree angle to the main portal, but there is no minaret, courtyard or side halls.

On entering through the high portal, one walks past a corridor and enters a single square and domed room with a basement. The arabesque detailing on the dome with tiles in shades of blue is one of the most exquisite seen in mosques of Iran. The interior too is decorated with riveted tilework in floral designs, shimmering in the light streaming in through the screened windows. Some consider this to be the most balanced interior in all Persian architecture. An unusual feature is the outlining of the arches with a tight cable-like tiling, separating yet integrating the dome component with the lower part of the structure from which the cupola rises.

SHAH MOSQUE (IMAM MOSQUE)

The more monumental of the two mosques abutting the Maidan is the Shah Mosque, later renamed the Imam Mosque after the Islamic Revolution in Iran in the late twentieth century. This mosque took almost twenty years to build, from AD 1611-30, and was later embellished with alabaster dados in AD 1638. It was built to replace the old Jami Mosque as the centre for congregational prayer.

The mosque is entered through a two-storeyed portal aligned to the Maidan but like the Lutfullah mosque, the main structure is set at a 45-degree angle to the entrance gateway, in order to face Mecca. The Shah Mosque received handsome

A medley of designs on the Shah Mosque dome.
Facing page: (top) A view of the decorated wall of the Sheikh Lutfullah Mosque; *(bottom)* The dome of the Lutfullah Mosque covers a single room and basement. The room is aligned with the qibla and contains a mihrab.

Aerial view of the Shah Mosque.
Facing page: Pishtaq or monumental main entrance of the Shah Mosque.

endowments from large commercial and agricultural properties attached to it by the Shah.

In plan, the mosque is not any different from others in Iran. It includes the courtyard, an iwan on each side, the qibla and a dome over the vaulted prayer hall. The plan is made more complex by several accretions – the madrassas with arcaded courtyards, the service areas for large numbers of pilgrims and visitors, and the vaulted winter-time prayer halls on either side of the domed prayer hall.

There are two pairs of minarets, one at the entrance portal and the other at the entrance to the prayer hall through a flat domed chamber. Inordinately high, these were not used to call the faithful to prayer. The call rang out from an arched recess over the western iwan, termed a guldasta in Persian – a common feature in later mosques.

Following the exuberant style of coloured tiling in Persia, the Shah Mosque too stands out for its decorative richness. The entire surface of the gateway is embedded with mosaic tiles in glowing blues, yellows, greens, white and black against a biscuit background. Calligraphy and the same cable binding as at the Lutfullah Mosque act as borders in the iwans. The motifs, in perfect harmony with one another, include flowers and vines, peacocks and other birds, and copies of prayer mats.

None of the other historic mosques built after the Shah Mosque of Isfahan equals its splendour. Only a few preceding it still capture the imagination in their totality, while some, such as the Nasir al-Mulk Mosque, built in Shiraz in the latter half of the nineteenth century, are attractive only in details of decoration. The Great Mosque of Goharashad in Mashad was built in the fifteenth century by the wife of Timur's eldest son Shahrukh. Goharashad was by all accounts a powerful personality and a patron of the arts. Bordered by two beautiful minarets, this mosque has a four-iwan courtyard surrounded by two-storeyed galleries all round, which were used for teaching. A minbar made of walnut wood without the use of any nails, is another of its outstanding features.

The beauty of Persian mosques lies in the sumptuousness of their surface decoration with tilework, and in that unique architectural innovation – the iwan. It has been remarked that one of the practical disadvantages of the iwan was that it contributed to overcrowding as people used the gigantic portals to shelter from the sun or rain. Further, the lodgings and madrassas usually attached to Persian mosques also led to large numbers of people congregating inside at any one point of time.

After Shah Abbas no other ruler had the money or the time to concentrate on buildings in Isfahan. The Hakim Mosque is one of the surviving few but it was funded by a Mughal donation from India. A few mosques were built in some other main cities, such as Shiraz in the south. However, the outstanding contribution of these, as in all Persian mosques, was decorative. Along with the rich and colourful tilework, calligraphy was raised to extraordinary heights of beauty and delicacy through the hands of the most famous calligrapher of the time, Ali Riza yi-Abbassi. More than architecture, it was in miniature paintings and book illustration that Persian artistic culture excelled.

Samarkand, the splendid Timurid city, where Bibi Khanum's Mosque stands against
the backdrop of the high arched portals of the Registan Square.

CHAPTER 9

Central Asia

Central Asia was traditionally the home of nomadic tribes periodically overrun by conquerors from east and west. As dynasties changed, caravan trails led to virgin land being converted into cities and towns. Culture and economy flourished. Caravanserais, tombs, madrassas and mosques were built. Genghis Khan, one of the world's greatest conquerors, was born here in AD 1167, the son of a petty Mongol chieftain or khan. Before he died in AD 1227 he had become the Great Khan and ruled from the China Sea to the borders of present-day eastern Europe. His descendants fanned out further westward into Iran, Anatolia and Baghdad and adopted Islam. One branch founded the Ilkhanid empire in Persia with its capital at Tabriz; another converted to Buddhism, the prevailing faith in Mongolia. By the mid-twelfth century Islam had been adopted by parts of the Turko-Mongol population. The Turkish Uighurs in northwest China too converted to Islam between the fourteenth and seventeenth centuries.

After Genghis Khan, Timur, 'Ruler of the World', dominates the history of the region. A man who killed thousands and destroyed complete cities, he also built one of the largest mosques in the world at Samarkand.

The artists, craftsmen and builders, and the spoils of conquest that Timur brought back, were used to make buildings that would dazzle the world with their scale and magnificence. Curiously, the gardens and suburbs he made were named after the places ravaged by him. Timurid architecture is an eclectic mix of the styles of all these different places. It is riveting because of its monumental scale and excessive splendour – colossal portals flanked by equally massive supporting pillars, external domes on high drums and often, long tapering minarets. Brick was the basic building material.

However, since they were structurally not built to withstand the seismic vulnerability of the region, not much has survived. The most outstanding mosque in Samarkand is the Bibi Khanum (AD 1399-1404). It covered an area of 460 x 325 feet (99 metres), the arch of the entrance portal spanning 62 feet (19 metres), behind which the dome overshadowed the building, reaching a height of 144 feet (44 metres). Timur is reported to have imported elephants from India to carry the huge blocks of stone for the Bibi Khanum Mosque and to have personally supervised its construction. Court poets of the time compared the dome to the vault of heaven and the portal's arch to the Milky Way. By all standards, it was a monumental structure, almost matched in scale by the later Kalan Friday mosque in Bukhara, which had a total of 288 domes and a monumental maqsura. Only its minaret has survived.

Timur's imperial architecture reflected his own ego and amassed wealth. During the rule of his grandson Ulugh Beg, a mathematician and astrologer, and other successors, no significant mosque was built, but the architecture of madrassas and mausoleums became more balanced in its proportions and decoration, as the Safavid phase began in Iran, and the era of the Great Mughals dawned in India.

Islamic Decoration

The architecture of Islam is embellished with a variety of decorative details, including engraving, tiles, reliefs, painting, calligraphy or gilding. The three-dimensional muqarnas, a uniquely Islamic feature, was used as a decoration on niches, domes, entrance portals, capitals and other surfaces. Islamic tenets frowned upon figural representation and a typical style developed using vegetal and abstract, mainly geometric, patterns and colour.

The use of ceramic and glass tiles was prominent, especially in Turkey, Iran and Central Asia. Turquoise and cobalt blue, yellow, black, brown, gold and green glazes, as also brilliantly hued semi-precious stones, were typically used in intricate mosaic designs. The patterns, depicting stylized flowers and vines in a technique that came to be known as arabesque, described the design of a continuous stem, splitting in rhythmic, repetitive patterns, emphasizing the infinity and oneness of the Islamic vision. The Mongol court in Iran adopted many Chinese floral motifs, while seventeenth-century Mughal craftsmen were inspired by European botanical drawings, which they transposed on to marble, using intricate inlay work. Simple geometric shapes were popular because of their aniconic quality. Arabic inscriptions from the Koran, in different scripts (Kufic, Nakshi, etc), highlighted the main architectural elements such as arches, domes or bases of minarets.

The element of light was used to accentuate spaces, colour and decoration. Wood and stone carving and patterned brickwork were common. The design of perforated screens (jaalis) reached their zenith in the mosques and buildings of Muslim rulers in India. They performed both a decorative and practical function as they formed intricate patterns of light and shade and allowed the circulation of air.

The Indian Subcontinent

The Arabs arrived on the western coast of the Indian subcontinent in the early eighth century. This invasion was, however, of little architectural consequence as the earliest footprints of Islam in India have all but been obliterated either by natural causes or by the looting of the entire seacoast by the Ghaznavids and Ghurids (minor dynasties from the region of Afghanistan), who followed in the eleventh and twelfth centuries. Their coming opened the subcontinent to the influences of Persia and Central Asia, giving rise to a new and refreshing era of Islamic architecture in this region.

The confrontation that took place between two established and vastly opposite cultures – indigenous Hindu and foreign Islamic – resulted in a unique spirit of mutual exchange. This manifested itself through a process of assimilation in the artistic, intellectual and social ethos without diluting the integrity and vigour of either side. Distance from the caliphate in Baghdad was an advantage, leaving the sultans, in their new capital at Delhi, free to encourage both secular and religious activities. Urban planning, commerce, architecture, music and literature were positively impacted.

While it is true that the eighth and ninth century Arabs bequeathed the earliest mosque in the subcontinent at a place called Bhambore in the Indus valley, only the statistical details of this historic monument are apparent in its excavated ruins. Four hundred years later, a Turkish slave, Qutb ud-din Aibak, who had risen to the rank of a viceroy in Mahmud Ghuri's conquered territories, was the builder of the first mosque of any significance in India. In AD 1192, Qutb ud-din stormed into Delhi and established himself at Qila Rai Pithora, the imperial capital of the Rajput ruler, Prithviraj Chauhan.

Carving detail on the Qutb Minar. *Facing page:* **An imposing arched screen was added to the Quwwat ul-Islam Mosque to counter the effect of the Hindu temple columns which were reused here.**

Delhi, situated at the mouth of the corridor between the foothills of the Himalayas and the fringes of the great Thar desert of Rajasthan, was the ideal location for defending India against foreign invasions along the northwest land route. Moreover, it was the focus of commercial and trading activity generated by the great hinterland of the Doab lying between the Ganga and the Yamuna rivers. Qutb ud-din's first concern, however, was not with trade and commerce. The undisputed power of the sword of Islam had now to be consolidated through the efforts of its builders.

QUWWAT UL-ISLAM MOSQUE, DELHI

True to the Prophet's dictate of installing a place of worship for the faithful on conquered territory, Qutb ud-din decided to build the Quwwat ul-Islam (literally, Power of Islam) Mosque in AD 1193 within the fortified city of Qila Rai Pithora. This was easier planned than implemented. The Ghurid forces were military and lacked builders, artisans and masons. Building the mosque was imperative, however, and the task had to be completed rapidly. Under the circumstances, the Muslims had to utilize local skills.

Thus, right at the inception of Islamic building activity in India, a joint venture between the Hindu builders and Islamic overseers became inevitable. Fortunately, the task of explaining the basic concepts of mosque design was simple, unlike temple design, which was governed by esoteric geomantic theories of architecture. The Prophet's House Mosque at Medina served as the prototype. A rectangular space with an open-to-sky courtyard, the basic mosque was enclosed by walls or cloisters on three sides, with a covered prayer hall on the western side, towards the direction of Mecca, indicated through the presence of the qibla and mihrab.

By the end of the twelfth century, Islamic architecture had built up an identifiable structural vocabulary. The two dominant elements were the arch and the hemispherical dome for roofing. In India, because of the need for speedy construction of the first congregational mosque, the warriors of the faith had perforce to look for building materials in the temples they destroyed in their iconoclastic zeal. These had been assembled out of meticulously cut structural elements such as beams, columns and lintels and put together without mortar. They were easy to dismantle but profusely carved with images of the pantheon of Hindu deities. The quick defacement of these figurative representations and their reorganization around a rectangular court resulted in the essential rudiments of the Quwwat ul-Islam Mosque – a colonnade around an open-to-sky courtyard. Moreover, the existing foundations of the Hindu sanctuary were made use of, with the western verandah being enlarged into a more spacious pillared hall. The rear wall of this hall was then adorned with the traditional qibla arch to guide the faithful to pray in the direction of Mecca.

The Quwwat ul-Islam Mosque originally covered 217 x 150 feet (66 x 46 metres). The extra height required, as at the corners, was achieved by superimposing one column over the other. To reinforce the Islamic element in the mosque, Qutb ud-din added an arched screen in AD 1198 on the western wall in front of the sanctuary. The huge central arch, 50 feet (15 metres) high, flanked on both sides by two smaller arches, was made by the method of corbelling. This technique served the purpose as the arch was instituted here only as a decorative, and not load-bearing, element. Finally, the rough

Facing page: In order to gain height, columns from Hindu temples were superimposed on one another in the trabeate form of construction.

rubble masonry was covered with red sandstone, richly carved with floral and calligraphic designs, another adaptation of local skills by Islamic patrons. Unlike the Persian use of brilliant multi-colour mosaic tile in decoration, Indian artists were more inclined towards subtler monochromatic carved surfaces.

In AD 1199, the foundations of the towering sandstone minaret (Qutb Minar) were laid just outside the mosque, as a fitting symbol of the might of Islam and the power of its patron. Starting from a base of 47 feet (14 metres) in diameter, it was destined to rise to a staggering height of 238 feet (73 metres), tapering to a width of 9 feet (2.7 metres), the top

storey being approached by a central spiral staircase of 360 steps. In the Arabic tradition of towers attached to mosques, like those of the Ibn Tulun Mosque at Cairo and the Great Mosque at Samarra, the minaret here formed an adjunct to the Quwwat ul-Islam mosque. It was an independent monument, which could be used to call the faithful to prayer and also serve the military function of a watchtower, below which the scarp of the Aravalli range was visible for miles around.

Aibak's son Iltutmish enlarged the mosque three times between AD 1210 and 1229 in order to include the great minaret in its courtyard. This area was again tripled in size about seventy years later by a subsequent ruler, Alauddin Khalji, to measure 748 x 443 feet (228 x 135 metres).

In a rather unprecedented manner, Iltutmish had appointed his daughter, Sultana Raziya, to succeed him as ruler of the Delhi Sultanate. Although endowed with admirable leadership qualities, she had little time for the affairs of state, particularly building activity, being more preoccupied with her romance with an Abyssinian slave whom she appointed as governor. Her rule – a period of intrigue, debauchery, treachery and murder – was racked by rebellion.

Raziya was overthrown by Balban, another slave turned general, who had faithfully served his master Mahmud Ghuri. Balban's court was resplendent with all the trappings of pomp and style though he himself was free of the vices so common among monarchs of the time. All his virtues, however, could not prevent internal rebellion nor the invasions from the northwest, which became more and more frequent.

The Slave dynasty came to an end with Balban, whose tomb near the Qutb complex, though modest in size and in ruins, is nevertheless of radical importance to Islamic building history in India. Here, for the first time, a true arch was put together using tapering stones, a technique originally used by Roman engineers. Subsequent Muslim rulers were to use the true arch in innovative ways to give the architecture of the subcontinent an essentially Indian character.

Delhi was ruled by a number of ineffectual kings after Balban, opening the way for the ascent of the Khalji dynasty. Alauddin Khalji, the third ruler, was as intensely pious as he was cruel, yet his court at Delhi attracted a large number of luminaries such as the poet Amir Khusrau and the historian al

Baruni. Drunk with his early military successes, Khalji soon developed the attributes of a true megalomaniac, venturing into many grandiose and foolhardy projects. In his ambitious building efforts, he enlarged the Quwwat ul-Islam mosque by throwing another asymmetrically arranged cloister around the existing one. In the centre courtyard of the extension on the northern side, he laid the foundations of the Alai Minar, a minaret intended to be almost double the size of the original Qutb Minar. However, it was never completed because of his untimely death.

Khalji also built the Alai Darwaza, the only one of six such gateways to be completed along the outer walls of the mosque. The cubic mass of this building was softened by the introduction of latticed screens (jaalis) – forerunners of what the Mughals were later to elevate to great works of art. The jaali became a decorative architectural device to provide controlled illumination and ventilation for the large voluminous spaces that were desired by Muslim builders, in contrast to the small and dark cubicles of the Hindu temple. The first of these large spaces was assembled in the building of the Jamat Khana Mosque in Nizamuddin, Delhi (AD 1325). The mosque marks a major stage in the evolution of mosques in India, for here, for the first time, the liwan (prayer hall) becomes a composite rectangular hall, uninterrupted by columns.

MOSQUES OF THE TUGHLAQ DYNASTY – BEGUMPURI, KHIRKI AND KALAN

The Khaljis were followed by the Tughlaqs, one of the most prolific building dynasties of Delhi. The tempo of activity was initiated by the first ruler, Ghias ud-din Tughlaq's decision to build a new fortress city. He had developed a distinct notion of architecture more akin to military establishments than to seraglios of pleasure and places of worship. This tendency had developed since he had been governor of Dipalpur in Multan in northwestern India, which lay in the direct path of western invasions into the region.

Near the fort of Tughlaqabad, which Ghias ud-din made his capital for a brief period, is his own tomb. The latter heralds a distinct feature that continued to nourish Islamic architecture in India for centuries. This was the combination of the arched form of construction and the lintel and beam method. Redundant stone lintels were installed just below the springing of the arch, resulting in an elegant and effective device of designing openings. Another innovation during

Begumpuri Mosque, one of the first Indian mosques to use the monumental stone gateway at the entrance to the courtyard.

Tughlaq times was the placement of the symbolically rich Hindu element of the kalasa (finial) at the apex of the dome.

One of the successors of Ghias ud-din, Feroze Shah Tughlaq, was the prince of builders. He is credited by some as having built forty mosques. His city, the fourth of Delhi's famed seven cities, was the first Muslim one to be built on the banks of the River Yamuna. Among the most characteristic of the numerous mosques of this period in Delhi are the Khirki and Kalan mosques (AD 1375) and the Begumpuri Mosque (AD 1370). Common to all is their militaristic style. This, however, was not achieved by building sloping, buttressed walls for the entire structure, but by locating the buttresses only at the corners, at the rear of the prayer hall facade and at the entrance points. The liwan had bays of stone columns and Tudor arches but a more prominent symbol of militarism was the massive arched and buttressed pylon-like structure invariably planted in the middle of this façade, equivalent to the Persian iwan.

Another design device that added to the grandeur of the Tughlaq mosques was the building of the courtyard over a platform or basement, often raised more than 12 feet (3.6 metres) above ground level. It necessitated the building of wide flights of steps leading to the entrance gateway, echoing the form of the central pylon dominating the sahn or courtyard. The lower level of the erected basement was marked by deep arched niches, generous enough in size to be put to use either as living rooms for mosque attendants and pilgrims, or as shops.

All the mosques of the Tughlaq period, except the Khirki Mosque, fall into this general pattern, varying only in size and details. In the Khirki Mosque is seen a style hitherto unknown

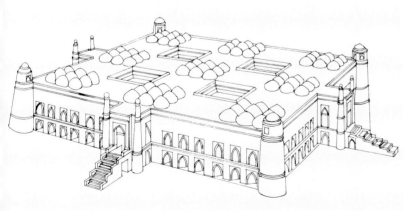

One of the two mosques of India where the courtyard was covered, the Khirki Mosque's prayer hall received little light, unlike the other three sides where light streamed in from perforated screen windows. *Facing page:* **Plan of the Jami Mosque at Gulbarga.**

to India. Here, driven by the need for shelter from the scorching summer sun, a part of the sahn was covered by a combination of half domes and a flat roof, leaving four symmetrically arranged open-to-sky courtyards for light and ventilation. Unfortunately, this device divided the space of the open courtyard into definable small spaces, and this compartmentalization of congregational worship became perhaps more unacceptable than the hot Indian sun. The style was repeated only once again at Gulbarga in south India. The choice was either to build the uninterrupted huge domed spaces of the Turkish mosques or be content with open courtyards. The latter remained the dominant element in the design of the Indian mosque.

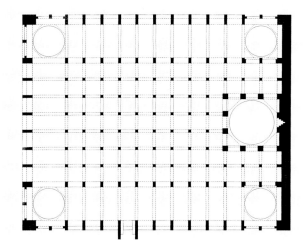

JAMI MOSQUE, GULBARGA

While builders in the north, east and western provinces of India were evolving an Indian Islamic style by grafting together local and borrowed traditions, a new idiom was evolving in the south. Muhammad Tughlaq (second in line after Ghias ud-din), during his mad venture of shifting the capital from Delhi to south central India in AD 1338, had sown the seeds of the earliest mosques in this region – the Jami Mosque at Daulatabad and the Deval Mosque at Bodhan. But the Tughlaq architectural style did not take firm root in the southern peninsula. Of these two mosques, while the mosque at Daulatabad was produced entirely with materials from temples in its vicinity, the one at Bodhan was merely a Jaina temple converted to a mosque through a few structural additions made to it.

Various circumstances led to southern builders accepting novel building ideas from other Muslim countries rather than developing on indigenous sources. For one, Muslim cities in the south, such as Bidar, Bijapur and Golconda, were not built around live and thriving centres of Hindu culture. So the spoils in the form of readymade Hindu building materials were not easily available in fashioning new structures. Furthermore, voyages across the Arabian Sea had become fairly frequent and skilled immigrants from Persia, and also distant Turkey, now served the Muslim overlords in the south. The conservative Hindu south was thus injected with doses of an alien and powerful architectural style. The energy generated by this infusion culminated in the building of the Gol Gumbaz at Bijapur, a royal mausoleum which would boast the largest dome in in the world in the sixteenth century. But before this, a Deccan sultan, Bahman Shah, of Persian origin, having thrown off his allegiance to Delhi, was busy establishing his capital at Gulbarga in modern Karnataka State. He appears to have invited an architect from the north Persian town of Qazvin to infuse more refined details in the ponderous military architecture of his fortress city. Of all the

buildings built there, however, only the Jami Masjid remains, surrounded by a devastating emptiness today.

Rafi, the acclaimed architect of the Gulbarga Friday mosque (AD 1367), appears to have been inspired more by Muslim religious edifices in eastern Europe than by the traditions of his Persian home. At the back of his mind may have been the huge domed and vaulted basilicas that had been converted to mosques. He therefore decided to abandon the open-to-sky central courtyard and replace it with an entirely roofed-in, domed and pillared hall. Measuring a handsome 216 x 176 feet (66 x 54 metres) and consequently covering an area of 37,916 square feet (3,523 square metres) in plan, the mosque's central hall, which is roofed over with sixty-three small cupolas, allows for five thousand worshippers at a time. Four larger domes mark the corners of the building, while the sanctuary is crowned by a stately, stilted dome rising over a square clerestorey. The architectural flourishes of the Gulbarba mosque now became a part of the south Indian building vocabulary.

JAMI MOSQUE, BIJAPUR

Bijapur lies on a ridge between two rivers. The city is dominated by the massive Gol Gumbaz, which evokes the glory of the hundred-year reign of the Adil Shahi dynasty, founded when Gulbarga and Bidar declined as centres of

Liwan façade of the Jami Masjid, Bijapur. Below the central dome with the crescent finial are shallow domes hidden by the thick roof. *Facing page:* Plan of the Bijapur mosque.

power and their appointed governors declared independence from the parent dynasties. Yusuf Adil Khan was the founder (AD 1490). A man singularly free of any signs of bigotry, his court attracted learned men and artists from as far away as Persia and Turkey. Despite his interest in the arts, however, he himself was not able to build much – two small mosques made from the spoils of destroyed temples are part of the architecture of his lifetime. Nevertheless, his successors inherited his artistic zeal, with the result that Bijapur has some of the finest architecture of the period. The Jami Masjid is one example.

Begun in AD 1570 by Ali Adil Shah but not completed by him, the Jami Masjid is undoubtedly influenced by the classical spirit of the Gulbarga Mosque. The idea of a covered central court was discarded here and the slightly more fanciful ogee arch of the Gulbarga cloisters was transformed into a more stately and dignified one. The liwan has a central hemispherical dome rising over the mihrab. It covers nine central bays built over a richly ornamented square clerestory platform. The rest of the prayer hall is roofed over by shallow circular domes over square bays formed by masonry piers.

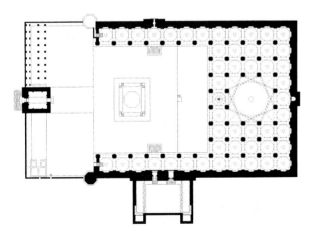

Seven stately arches in the façade of the liwan are shaded by a deep horizontal chajja (parapet), supported by a row of closely spaced brackets. Usually, the exterior in mosques of the time would be formed of large blank masonry walls surrounding the liwan and the side wings. In this mosque, these surfaces are cleverly contrived as a double row of deep arched niches, the lower one being blind, and the upper admitting light and air into the liwan.

It is, however, in the interior of the liwan that the mosque achieves an air of solemnity, much like that in the mosque of Mandu, with its white plastered surfaces ornamented with deep grooved bands, and offset by robust masonry piers that are spanned by low arches. The mihrab is ornamented with architectural motifs and calligraphy, a niche within a niche in subtle colours giving a *trompe l'oeil* effect. During Mughal emperor Aurangzeb's time, part of the flooring was divided into 2,250 prayer rug-like rectangular compartments.

Aurangzeb lived in Bijapur for some years in the late seventeenth century but when it was ceded to the Marathas in AD 1724, the wealth of materials in the city's public buildings was ruthlessly stripped away, including woodwork, doors and windows. Despite this, and even in its derelict splendour today, the remains of the handiwork of the short-lived Adil Shahi dynasty point to their genius in building.

ATALA MOSQUE, JAUNPUR

Despite the regional peculiarities of geography and customs, the various provincial outposts of Islam echoed Delhi as centres of political intrigue. As kings, ministers and usurpers grasped and sustained power in provinces such as Jaunpur, Mandu and Bengal, they simultaneously conspired to hold

both temporal and religious power. Democracy and authoritarianism were alternately eschewed and though there was frequent conflict between the ruler and the Muslim religious head, it was not sharp enough to discourage the former from financing the building of mosques and self-glorifying tombs. The number of mosques built was, however, small, for despite being the acknowledged state religion, Islam was not able to command universal following among the Indian people, who had been steeped in the Hindu faith for centuries. Nevertheless, it was politically imperative that mosques be quickly built in order to establish the new faith.

The earliest provincial mosques are also no more than a recomposition of building materials rescued from existing Hindu and Jaina temples. Most merely followed the model established at Delhi. The most captivating style was seen in Jaunpur, a province of the Delhi Sultanate, located only 58 kilometres southeast of the holy city of Varanasi. Said to have been built by Feroze Shah Tughlaq in AD 1360, it was natural that the militaristic style of the Tughlaq rulers should serve as the inspiration. Three significant mosques have survived from this period.

The earliest is the Atala Mosque, built in AD 1408. Its name derives from a temple to the goddess Atala Devi, which stood on the site and was destroyed to make way for the mosque. Its most attractive feature is the inevitable but robust design of the central opening of the liwan. The circular tapering shafts of the Tughlaq military model are now resolved into rectangular turrets while retaining the inclined profile of the original. The wavering and ornamental ogee arch of the Tughlaqs also gives way to a huge arch suspended between the two rectangular turrets – more purposeful and majestic in its firm outline. Typical Hindu bracketed openings find their

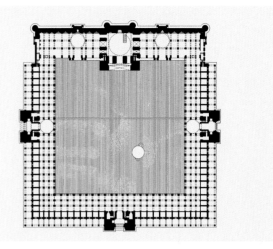

place, as usual, at the base of the arch, its upper reaches being filled in with arched apertures, jharokhas (balconies) and jaalis. Quite aware of the dramatic quality of this central entranceway, the builders of the Atala Mosque installed two identical smaller pylons on either side of it, and also three gateways in the centres of the eastern, northern and southern colonnades of the courtyard.

Inscriptional evidence testifies to the fact that the Atala Mosque was the work of a Hindu architect, a telling detail that points to the pluralistic climate of cultures that was made possible through architecture.

The other two Jaunpur mosques are the Jami Mosque, that took about forty years to complete, and the small Lal Darwaza Mosque. The Jami Mosque's square courtyard alone is larger than the entire mosque of Atala. It was built over a raised platform, its courtyard surrounded on three sides by an unusual two-storeyed cloister, in proportion with the scale of the entire concept.

All three mosques display a design detail uniquely seen in Jaunpur – the separation of an elevated platform on either

Plan of Jaunpur's Atala Mosque, which was inspired by the architecture of Delhi.
Facing page: The Jami Mosque of Jaunpur was built between AD 1438-78 over a high platform, and a wide flight of steps has to be climbed to reach the lofty entrance and courtyard.

side of the minbar within the liwan, screened off by panels of jaali so that women could also participate, in purdah, in the ritual of worship within the mosque. This provision probably owes its origin to Bibi Raja, the queen of the ruler Mahmud Shah. She had the Lal Darwaza Mosque built probably as a private chapel attached to her palace. The women's enclosure remained a feature of the public mosques of Jaunpur.

JAMI MOSQUE, MANDU

Another picturesque Muslim province was that of Malwa in central India, with the twin capital cities of Dhar and Mandu. During Timur's sack of Delhi, Mahmud Tughlaq had sought refuge here. After Tughlaq returned to Delhi following

Timur's departure from India in AD 1401, its Afghan governor broke away from the Delhi Sultanate and made Dhar his capital. After his death, his son, Alp Khan Ghuri, succeeded him and shifted the capital to Mandu. Here he laid the foundations of one of the most dramatically sited fort citadels on the Vindhya range, overlooking the beautiful Narmada River. The site was a natural spur at an elevation of 2,000 feet (610 metres) above sea level and separated from mainland Malwa by a winding gorge. The fortress walls enclosed an area of approximately 334 square feet (31 square metres) and were 40 kilometres in circumference.

Alp Khan took on the title of Hushang Shah and proceeded to construct a variety of buildings. The Jami Masjid was begun by him but completed by a subsequent ruler. It is undoubtedly the most majestic building in Mandu; very few

In the Jami Mosque, Mandu, the minbar and dikka (reading platform) are about the only decorative elements.
Facing page: Mosque at Dholka, Gujarat, where the entrance elevation is identical to the assembly hall of a Hindu temple.

mosques in India, including those of the Great Mughals, can touch this one in its simplicity and sobriety. Even as it stands today, stripped of its gentler artifacts such as chhajjas and coloured stone decoration, its stately courtyard alone has an awesome presence. Said to be modelled on the Great Mosque at Damascus, the ambience of the mosque becomes apparent at the entrance itself, where a huge domed porch projects from the eastern façade on to a broad, stately flight of steps. The doorway is embellished with carved jaali screens and bands of blue enamel tiles. As one passes under the high vaulted porch, the great courtyard opens out, surrounded on three sides by a uniformly proportioned colonnade with majestic arches, with just a hint of the ogee at the apex. Above these are planted cylindrical cupolas of a distinctively masculine order. These rise vertically from their circular base to converge near the apex. Larger ones of the same stately profile are planted at the corners of the mosque, while crowning the skyline is a massive and strikingly handsome dome over the centre of the liwan, making a total of 158 domes for this mosque. Considering the overall size of the square building – 288 feet (88 metres) on each side – the domes are perhaps not too many.

The Jami Mosque announces its sacred intent in its assemblage of solemn and silent spaces, a work of considerable power, more eloquent in its simplicity than many other elaborate mosques of the Islamic world.

The two great domes of the Jami Mosque were aligned with that of a madrassa in front of the eastern entrance, where later a royal tomb was built. On the western side, the domes were aligned with the central dome of the adjacent tomb complex of Hushang Shah. The three structures create a grand and unified composition.

MOSQUES OF GUJARAT

At first controlled through governors appointed from Delhi, Gujarat's local Muslim rulers declared independence by the end of the thirteenth century. Political liberty was, however, easier gained than architectural freedom – they could not overlook the highly evolved art established by local guilds of craftsmen and builders in Gujarat. This resulted in the adoption of the existing style of both structure and decoration. Profuse carving and a lavish volumetric scale was adapted in the architecture of mosques and tombs. The only innovation was that of the pointed arch.

The earliest Muslim building effort in Gujarat, begun soon after the raids of Alauddin Khalji at the end of the thirteenth century, was the Jami Masjid at Bharoach, an ancient and prosperous seaport. In this there was little time to indulge in architectural refinements and the building is a quick putting together of columns recovered from existing Hindu temples. These columns support corbelled domes, separated from each other by a flat-roofed aisle. The whole is enclosed by solid

masonry walls with tiny arched and trellised openings for ventilation. The critical eastern wall is sheltered by a typical Hindu chajja but otherwise left open.

A later Jami Mosque, built at Cambay, was an affront to the rich Jaina heritage of the region. It was an obvious plagiarisation of a Delhi model, with Islamic features such as domes and arches added on to rescued Hindu columns. The entrance gateway in the middle of the eastern cloister is virtually a re-erected temple portico with a dome added on for Islamic effect. Another pure imitation is seen in the mosque at Dholka (AD 1333), then a centre of importance and wealth in Gujarat. The gateway here is almost identical to the entrance mandapa (assembly hall) of a Hindu temple, and even includes the inclined seats seen along the periphery of the mandapa. Eighty years later, in the mosque of a dignitary, Sayyid Alam, built in Ahmedabad in AD 1412, the true prototype of future mosque architecture in Gujarat emerged. The mosque's façade contained porticoes on the sides, projecting cornices and ornamental brackets, together with a variety of decorative details, incorporating all the fineness of Gujarat's florid style.

In the Jami Mosque of Ahmedabad, completed in AD 1423, the religious architecture of two opposite beliefs seems to fuse on equal terms, lending and borrowing in a truly democratic spirit to make a rich blend. This is all the more surprising as the mosque's patron, Ahmed Shah, was one of the most bigoted of Muslim rulers. If he had realized that a temple building was being introduced into the mosque sanctuary, he would probably have ordered its demolition. Architecturally, in fact, the design gained by this fusion. Through the graceful Islamic arches of the main façade the interplay of light and shade could now be perceived between the slender columns

The Jami Mosque is among the very few buildings that have remained intact in Champaner. While the interior is distinguished by well articulated spaces, with balconies on the upper level for meditation, the exterior *(facing page)* displays the Gujarat ornamental trend to some extent with stone mouldings breaking the monotony of plain surfaces.

of the hall and the engrailed 'flying' arches connecting them, an element borrowed from the temple.

Inside the liwan of this mosque, there are about three hundred tall slender pillars, with a central open space rising vertically through two tiers of flanking balconies and roofed by a large corbelled dome resting over an octagonal rig of columns. Each of the eight sides is filled in with panels of jaalis. In one deft stroke of design, the builders had solved many functional problems of mosque design in Gujarat. The balconies provided a sufficiently private area for the women, the domed roof added a traditional element to the interior as well as the façade; and the open grills in the dome generated cool currents of air in the central shaft.

JAMI MOSQUE, CHAMPANER

Champaner, located about 113 kilometres southeast of Ahmedabad, had been a Hindu stronghold. It was captured by the Muslim potentate from Ahmedabad, Mahmud Beghara (AD 1458), under whose rule there was a frenzy of building activity. It took him a quarter of a century to build Champaner but it was inhabited only during his time. Now a desolate archaeological site, two of its mosques stand out, the more important being the Jami Mosque (AD 1523).

Its design is a marked development of its counterpart at Ahmedabad. The liwan façade here discards the open colonnade wings of the Ahmedabad prototype. The other sides of the prayer hall are ornamented with balconies, bracketed openings, turrets, buttresses and corner minarets singularly Hindu in ornamentation. Inside, however, the concept of a 'temple inside a mosque' is as predominant as in the Jami Mosque at Ahmedabad, which is a hypostyle hall

with a forest of columns. The centre of the hall, rising to a height of 65 feet (20 metres), has the impact of a domed nave. The surrounding balcony enclosing the rotunda is octagonal in its circumference, and the whole is surmounted by a ribbed and richly fretted dome rising on pillars. The galleries themselves, separated from the pillared prayer hall below, provide retreats for meditation.

The entire decorative scheme is purely geometric, with only a hint of more free flowing sculptural forms. In another fifty years, the Gujarat craftsman's skill was honed to perfection in the mosque of a nobleman, Siddi Sayyid, at Ahmedabad (AD 1572), surpassing in beauty even the rich ornamental treatment of the exterior of the Champaner mosque. In the Siddi Sayyid mosque, the ten arched apertures of the western walls of the liwan were carved in stone with exquisite tracery in the form of trees and turned into masterpieces of art, equalling the best of Mughal workmanship at Delhi or Agra.

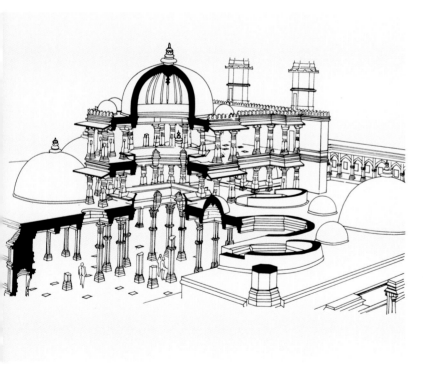

JAMI MOSQUE, FATEHPUR SIKRI

In AD 1571 the greatest of the Mughal emperors, Akbar (AD 1556-1605), found his way to Sikri, situated about 41 kilometres on a ridge west of Agra. Here, his grandfather, Babur, had waged a crucial war in the plains below and built a small mosque as a 'shukri' (thanksgiving) to celebrate his victory. Akbar had visited many Muslim saints to seek their intervention in his desire for a son and heir. In Sikri he found Sheikh Salim Chisti, who predicted the birth of three sons. The eldest, Salim (Jahangir), was born here, at the same time that Akbar was gaining victory after victory in Gujarat and Rajasthan. He therefore believed that Sikri was an auspicious site for a new capital; the ruins of buildings of earlier Rajput inhabitants also convinced him of its architectural potential.

Fatehpur Sikri (originally named Fathabad in Persian, or City of Victory) was planned in such a way that function, orientation, topography, security and aesthetics, each played a part. Public areas such as the courts, the Diwan-i-Am (Hall of Public Audience) and the Jami Mosque formed a ring around the private audience chambers of the royal residences, which were located at the very heart of the complex, astride the top of the ridge. Service areas, such as the waterworks, serais, and guards' quarters were located on the lower outskirts. Orientation was rigidly adhered to so all important structures were located along the cardinal axes. While buildings of a secular nature were installed along the north-south axis, the Jami Masjid was symmetrically erected, as required in India, around the east-west axis, facing Mecca. Overall visual unity was ensured primarily through the use of red sandstone for all the different parts of the building, including floors, lintels, beams, etc.

Jami Mosque of Fatehpur Sikri, set on the highest point of a ridge, is surrounded by local habitation. Salim Chisti's tomb shines like an iridescent pearl in one corner. *Facing page: (top)* A detail from the interior of a dome in Champaner; *(bottom)* The Jami Masjid, Champaner.

The Jami Mosque is located at the highest point of the ridge. It is an enormous building, the largest in the city, measuring 515 x 432 feet (157 x 132 metres). It took five years to build (the entire construction of Fatehpur Sikri took about ten years). The mosque was dedicated to Salim Chisti, who died just before it was completed in AD 1572. Its entrance from within the newly built capital was from the eastern gateway, the Badshahi Darwaza (royal gateway), beyond which lay the huge expanse of the courtyard.

The central arch of the entrance is said to be modelled on the one at Mecca. In the prayer hall are seven bays and three mihrabs, the central, pentagonal one being covered by a dome. On either side of the central chamber, three arches lead to aisles, with pillars in the Hindu style. The mosque's weakness is the liwan façade. This consists of a central arched gateway which dwarfs the dome behind (in the old Tughlaq tradition). Moreover, the arch is completely out of proportion to the rather low-slung side wings, which have vaguely organized arches of as many as three different spans and heights and are shaded by small sloping chajjas. However, the interior of the mosque evokes the sculptural grandeur of the rest of Sikri as it gives the appearance, in carefully carved stone, of a timber ribbed dome. Complementing the majesty of the structure, the parapets of the cloisters and liwan are embellished by a row of exquisitely domed chattris where torches would be lit at night during festive occasions.

To Akbar's visionary sense of aesthetics, the rather plebian nature of the mosque must have been a disappointment. He availed of every opportunity to impart some liveliness to the drab courtyard and its fortress-like walls. The tomb of a dignitary was placed in the northeastern corner of the courtyard and subsequently Salim Chisti was also buried here. His tomb stands out like a luminous pearl encased in red. Its verandah and dome were originally in red sandstone but later completely covered with white marble, exquisitely finished with marble screens and serpentine brackets by Akbar's son and heir Jahangir. Every day, in front of it, the haunting chorus of qawwali (Sufi music) singers rings out over the courtyard, compelling visitors to stop and listen to it entranced while they soak in the beauty of the mosque.

The crowning glory is the Buland Darwaza, a massive gateway in the southern wall of the mosque, built by Akbar to commemorate his victorious campaigns in the Deccan and Gujarat. Set within a frame of intentionally immense proportions, the actual entrance is of a modest size. However, the composition manages to maintain a fluid relationship between the rising of the great alcove above and the human scale at the base. The Buland Darwaza's resplendent arch (almost 50 feet [15 metres] wide and 100 feet [30 metres] high) evokes a feeling of both passage and shelter. The line of vision descends from its scalloped, semi-domed portal to the modest two-storeyed rows of arches and balconies set in pentagonal fashion at the base. The entrance is wide enough to accommodate attendants' rooms on either side. The transition from awesome monumentality to a humble and sheltered passageway, from wide open spaces outside the gateway to the sequestered courtyard within, is smoothly achieved. An inscription inside the entrance reads: "Jesus Son of Mary (on whom be peace) said: The world is a bridge, pass over it, but build no houses on it. He who hopes for an hour may hope for eternity. The world endures but an hour. Spend it in prayer, for the rest is unseen."

Facing page: The lofty Buland Darwaza in red sandstone with marble outlines is crowned by a line of small domed pavilions contrasting in scale with the massive arched entranceway.

In the tradition of Indian mosques, Sikri too is built on a platform, rising 42 feet (13 metres) above ground level and approached by a grand flight of steps that widens out at the base for structural strength. Soaring thin minarets frame the arched entrance, accentuating the verticality of the 134 feet (41 metres) high portal. On top is a merloned parapet and domed kiosks, without which no Mughal monument was complete. An interesting feature of Fatehpur Sikri is that while the mosque contains all the traditional elements of Muslim buildings, such as arches and domes, the secular buildings in the city are all of trabeate construction, typical of the Hindu building vocabulary.

Akbar lived in Fatehpur Sikri for fourteen years, and when it was abandoned, some say because of a shortage of water, he seldom returned here, probably because of his military and political preoccupations elsewhere.

JAMI MOSQUE, DELHI

The fifth Mughal emperor Shahjahan's 'reign of marble' (AD 1628-57) was a fitting climax to Mughal building activity in India. He set up high standards of design, workmanship and detail, with the Taj Mahal being a perfect climax to over four hundred years of Muslim architecture in India. During his time, three remarkable fort-citadels were built, at Lahore, Agra and Delhi, which included palaces, tombs, public buildings and mosques. Even before he could complete the Jami Mosque at Agra, however, the emperor's attention was focused

on his new capital in Delhi. Here the construction of the last of the great mosques of India was under way. The Jami Mosque in Delhi, begun in AD 1644, part of Shahjahan's capital city of Shahjahanabad, is the largest mosque in India, an appropriate climax to a tradition of mosque building that began with the Quwwat-ul-Islam, about five hundred years earlier, and saw the erection of subsequent mosques of a uniquely Indian character.

The Jami Mosque stands over a raised foundation, on a platform that is 325 feet (99 metres) on each side, overlooking the Red Fort citadel. The elevation necessitated the installation of broad flights of steps leading to impressive gateways in the tradition of the grand entrance portals of the mosques of Mandu and Jaunpur. The main gateway is on the eastern side. It opens out on to an immense red sandstone – flagged quadrangle of 325 feet (67 metres) side, in front of which stands the 220 x 90 feet (67 x 27 metres) mosque sanctuary. On the other three sides, ranges of cloisters extend their long colonnades, broken by gateways at the cardinal points. Shahjahan's elegant style of architecture is characterized here by the graceful onion domes of the mosque in white marble striped in red over the sanctuary, by the cusped arch gateway, and the tall vertically striped minarets.

A pair of slender minarets frame the vaulted entrance to the liwan, while the broader, three balconied ones flank the sides of the prayer hall. At the top of each of the corner towers is a graceful, airy pavilion, capped by a cupola and kalasa. The call to prayer rings out from here five times a day, across the dense settlement below of houses, shops, a bazaar of religious books and souvenirs, a wholesale fish market and narrow

A view of Old Delhi from the minaret of the Jami Mosque. *Following pages 126 & 127:* Delhi's grand mosque is more than a place for worship. It has become an important sightseeing destination as well as a community gathering place for the mainly Muslim neighbourhood that surrounds it.

alleys smelling of freshly cooked curries and pulaos. On Muslim festivals, the mosque and its surroundings are a riot of colour with balloons and streamers and families out in glittering new clothes.

The Jami Mosque is the true heart of Shahjahanabad. It took five thousand workmen over six years to build it. Perhaps this mosque lacks the air of gravity of the mosque at Mandu or the militaristic solidity of the Begumpuri Mosque in Delhi, but it is an architecturally lucid composition that has an air of grandeur more spectacular than any of its predecessors.

MOSQUES IN PAKISTAN

Large parts of the vast fertile plains of the Punjab, the Land of Five Rivers (the Indus and its tributaries) now belong to the modern state of Pakistan. It was from here that in the eleventh century, the first significant invasions into the Indian subcontinent were made by Afghan invader Mahmud of Ghazna. Multan, practically in the centre of Pakistan, was an important Islamic outpost. Surrounded by rich agricultural lands and nurtured by the river, it was endlessly ransacked by waves of invaders lured by its natural wealth. It was also a religious centre for pilgrims attracted to its ancient Sun Temple, which was destroyed six hundred years later by the orthodox Mughal emperor Aurangzeb. By the twelfth century, Lahore had become the most dazzling city in the Muslim subcontinent, before the invasions of another Afghan, Mahmud of Ghuri, in AD 1192, when it was replaced by Delhi.

In the Indus delta was built the earliest mosque of the Indian subcontinent at a place called Bhambore (earlier known as Daibul) in AD 727. It was a simple structure, modelled on the Friday mosque of Kufa in Iraq and part of a palace complex like the one at Al Mansura near Hyderabad, Sindh. Bhambore is believed to be the place where Islam was first introduced to the subcontinent by the Iraq general, Mohammad bin Qasim. Like Thatta, further inland, it was a prosperous port city.

Thatta flourished between the fourteenth and seventeenth centuries, until the shifting course of the Indus, 80 kilometres further eastwards, resulted in its decline. Nevertheless, one of the most beautiful mosques, begun by emperor Shah Jahan and almost completed by Aurangzeb, is located here. Extensive renovations by the government in recent times have restored this mosque to its original splendour. Surmounted by innumerable domes, the centre vault is completely and intricately covered with delicate mosaic tiles in shades of turquoise, rust, brown and black. Tilework also delineates the arches and interior of the dome in geometric designs. The arched colonnades are constructed with meticulous brickwork, offset at particular points with designs in turquoise tiles.

BADSHAHI MOSQUE, LAHORE

Studded with a fort, mosques, mausoleums and gardens, and nurtured by the warmth of its people and a sophisticated culture, Lahore well deserved the accolade 'pearl of the Punjab'. During its golden age of Mughal glory, it attracted scholars, musicians, writers and mystics in large numbers.

The first Mughal emperor Babur's son Kamran, though governor of Kabul and Kandahar, was allowed to rule over Lahore, which he beautified with gardens and pavilions.

Akbar, third in line in the Mughal dynasty, made Lahore his capital. Insatiably curious and a man ahead of his time, Akbar propounded his own universal religion, Din-i-Ilahi, which included elements from sources as diverse as Islam and Christianity, pantheism and astrology. His restless spirit drove him to enlarge his empire and consolidate affairs of state. He moved his capital several times, between Lahore, Delhi and Fatehpur Sikri.

During his fifty-year rule, when Thatta and Sind were brought into the fold of his empire, Lahore was his capital from AD 1584 for fourteen years. His most important contribution architecturally was to fortify the city and build the beautiful Diwan-i-Am and Diwan-i-Khas inside the fort. The oldest surviving mosque in the city dates to his reign, having been built by his wife Miriam Zamani, mother of Jahangir. It is delicately frescoed, and was unfortunately used by the Sikhs as a powder magazine when they occupied it during the eighteenth and nineteenth centuries.

Most of the important buildings in the Lahore fort, however, belong to Akbar's grandson, Shahjahan, the most prolific of the Mughal builders. These include a grand entrance gate with steps wide enough to accommodate elephants. He also built the Shah Burj or Royal Palace, where the famous Kohinoor Diamond is reputed to have been handed over to the British.

Shahjahan was deposed by his son Aurangzeb in AD 1657, who also put to death his brother Dara Shikoh, heir apparent to the emperor and a prince who had endeared himself to the people of Lahore. A rigid believer of Islam, Aurangzeb enforced the Sharia law on all his subjects, antagonizing non-believers, because of which he had to move away from Delhi to the relative security of Lahore. Here he built the most outstanding of Mughal monuments in the city – the Badshahi Mosque.

The mosque has all the characteristics of Mughal architecture of the subcontinent. It is monochromatic, being built of brick but dressed with red sandstone. Only its domes and cupolas are in white marble. It stands on a high plinth covering a 558-feet (170-metre) square area, its main arched entrance approached by a wide sweep of stairs. A total of 53 minarets, each a metre high, adorn all the corners. The prayer hall is relatively small but has massive arches perfectly proportioned to carry the load of the three main domes above. The mihrab is also in white marble. The walls around the courtyard originally housed study rooms but were later demolished by the British for security reasons and arcaded.

The Badshahi Mosque is modelled on the Friday mosques of Delhi and Agra but is larger than either of these. It can hold up to sixty thousand worshippers, who, during Eid prayers, spread out over the gardens that surround it. Immediately opposite its eastern entrance is the Alamgiri Gate of the Fort, which was rebuilt by Aurangzeb in order to align it with the eastern wall of the mosque.

Aurangzeb's strength of character and industrious habits helped him to remain in the saddle for almost half a century – longer than any of the Mughal emperors. Orthodoxy drove him to construct religious buildings but the bigoted pursuit of Islamic practices did not allow him the imaginative creativity of his predecessors. The architecture of his time was a mere and poor imitation of his father's sensuous style and with him, not only did the Mughal dynasty disintegrate rapidly, but the grand history of great mosque building in India also came to an end.

The Badshahi Mosque, built by Aurangzeb, exceeded in size even the Jami Mosque of Delhi on which it was modelled.
Its marble domes are in striking contrast to the monochromatic red sandstone in which it was built.

The Ulema and Madrassa

There is no priestly class in Islam. Any Muslim conversant with the Koran and the prescribed rituals can lead the congregation in prayer. During the Umayyad caliphate this duty was performed by the caliphs, who were the religious as well as secular heads of state. This role was gradually taken over by governors and senior political appointees. As the class of learned scholars grew, the ruler distanced himself from the details of religious affairs, though he remained a patron of mosques, madrassas (centres of Islamic learning) and other religious activities. The ulema (the word derives from 'ilm' meaning knowledge) comprised religious and legal scholars, who interpreted the Koran and the sunna (the Prophet's words and deeds) and prescribed the way a good Muslim should live, according to the Sharia or laws developed by them. Mosques soon became centres of instruction in Islamic jurisprudence, with independent lodgings and madrassas being established in their proximity.

The ulema were also entrusted by the state to conduct marriage and burial ceremonies, to maintain the legal system as qazis (law givers) and supervise charitable activities. The imam or leader of the local Muslim community led the prayers in his neighbourhood mosque, while those of larger, state mosques, could exercise their authority beyond the scope of religious activities to a wider community.

The madrassa as an institution developed in the tenth century under the Sunni Seljuks, who zealously propagated Islam and found it a useful means of countering the Shiite interpretations of the doctrine. Not only theology, but jurisprudence, administration, political sciences, languages and literature were taught. These early schools were funded and maintained by endowments from the income of state-owned real estate. Staff and students were supported with generous scholarships. Merv, Herat, Nishapur and Baghdad were among the first places where madrassas were founded. From here they spread to Mesopotamia, Syria and Palestine and on to Egypt, where the Mamluks were great patrons of the institution.

The madrassa often included the tomb of the founder and also charitable components such as a hospital, kitchen or elementary school. The founder and his heirs were the trustees of the property, which ensured that it remained within the family, for charitable institutions could not be taken over by the state.

CHAPTER 11

Contemporary Mosques

As Arab and other traders plied the Silk Road in the north of the Asian continent and sea routes to its south, Islam reached its far corners. While the earliest known mosque in China is believed to have been built in the seventh century AD in Guangzhou, it was only in the fifteenth century that in the northern Xinjiang region of the country Islam became the main religion. Mosque architecture in China ranges in style from the Central Asian to the traditional Chinese, with pagoda roofs and profuse external wood carved and painted ornamentation.

In Southeast Asia, the island archipelago of present-day Indonesia (Java, Sumatra, Kalimantan) was introduced to Islam by traders and wandering mystics from India between the twelfth and fifteenth centuries. Hindu-Buddhist by tradition, these places accepted more readily the Sufi aspects of the religion, which were incorporated into local customs. Today Indonesia has the largest Muslim population in the world.

With the weakening of the Ottoman empire towards the beginning of the nineteenth century, the era of European colonization began, resulting in great changes in society all over the world. European norms were adopted by the elite. At the same time, as traditional and religious values were threatened, communities became more entrenched in their own identities.

In Banda Aceh in Indonesia, one of the oldest Islamic cities in Southeast Asia, an old mosque, rebuilt by the Dutch, exhibits the typically hybrid vocabulary of the period. Located on the northwestern tip of Sumatra, Banda Aceh was the gateway through which traders from Gujarat first brought Islam to Indonesia. Fundamental Islamic elements such as the dome and minaret are used in the mosque here, along with recognizable colonial features such as wide portico-like verandahs with arches and sloping tiled roofs. The first section of the present structure of the mosque was built by

A detail from Banda Aceh mosque in Indonesia. *Facing page:* Employing several forms, techniques and styles executed with superior craftsmanship, the walls, ceiling, floors and structural supports of the Mosque of Hassan II are all splendidly decorated.

133

the Dutch in AD 1879 after the original one had burnt down and, in the course of the next century, several domes and turrets were added. The mosque survived the devastation left by the tsunami in December 2004.

As independence movements gained momentum after the First World War, new nations were formed. Islam remained the religion of the majority in several of these countries, which adopted major modernization programmes in governance, education, and other social systems. Rapid increases in population necessitated ambitious urban development programmes. The environment of towns and cities has changed radically in the modern age, and even in the heartland of Islam, Saudi Arabia, the phenomenal increase in wealth due to soaring petrol prices has resulted in a changed landscape of mega malls, housing colonies, new airports and hotels.

Among the new buildings, the mosque has established a strong presence as Muslim communities transit across the globe. Patronage has changed to the state or community and sometimes, individuals of wealth. The architectural idiom is now more cross-cultural, often boldly so, as seen in the White Mosque in Bosnia. These changes are a response to the accessibility of new materials and design ideas. At the same

time, a historicist extravagance with traditional form and decoration, as in the Bhong Mosque, Pakistan, or experiments in the adaptation of vernacular forms, as in New Gourna, Egypt, are resulting in buildings that seek to reconcile the past with the present.

SHEREFUDDIN'S WHITE MOSQUE, VISOKO, BOSNIA

Visoko lies north of Sarajevo in the valley of the Bosna River. It was a centre of trade in the late medieval period when Bosnia was an independent kingdom. Its Muslim heritage goes back to the Ottoman period between the fifteenth and nineteenth centuries. Despite the socialist system of

governance it later adopted, its approximately thirty thousand-strong Muslim community retained its identity, with the architecture of the town also following the Islamic Ottoman style. The dramatically abstract form of the Sherefuddin White Mosque, built in 1980, is thus a breakaway statement of a religious community willing to accept change and move boldly with the times.

In 1967, the Muslim community decided to build a central mosque in place of an earlier one. They asked a well-known teacher and architect, Zlatko Ugljen, to design it for them. He provided his services free of charge and the community voluntarily contributed the major part of the funds.

The mosque is built in concrete and is the focal point of an existing complex of shops, houses and a graveyard, in the style of the Turkish kulliye. Traditionally, Ottoman and, therefore, Bosnian mosques incorporated memorial gardens and tombs for important and saintly persons. The graveyard here lies adjacent to the prayer hall on the east but shut off from it by a solid wall. The road to the mosque slopes down to the entrance and prayer hall, protectively cradled in a hollow. This location gives it both privacy and protection from the chilling Bosnian winters. A see-through glass panel separates the prayer hall from the courtyard, allowing natural light and a sense of continuity. Inside is a simple, white, unadorned space, with an abstract representation of the mihrab as a niche inset with a pinewood composition. A depressed central section of the carpeted prayer hall and soft lighting through skylights add depth to the pristine interior.

Though traditional in design, the Bhong Mosque reflects the flamboyant visual culture of the Punjab region in Pakistan.
Facing page: (top) **Abstract pyramidical forms make a bold sculptural statement in Sherefuddin's White Mosque, Bosnia;**
(bottom) **Liquorice-coloured domes shine against the white surfaces of the mosque in Banda Aceh.**

BHONG MOSQUE, PAKISTAN

Located in a village of about five thousand inhabitants, the Bhong Mosque in the Punjab region is a work of pure craftsmanship. No architect was employed to design this mosque, modelled on the Mughal architecture of India. It was a labour of love, conceived by a wealthy landlord in 1932 and completed by his son, Rais Ghazi Muhammad, in 1983.

The mosque was planned as part of a larger infrastructural development project for the village, which would include building roads, providing electricity, irrigation and public transport, and generating employment. The mosque and the library occupy an elevated and focal position in the building complex, which includes three large residential areas and a madrassa. The house of the founding family of Rais Ghazi is part of the complex. An earlier smaller mosque that stood on the site is now used exclusively for women.

Minaret-like towers, capped with jharokhas and cupolas, buttress the mosque on all sides. The actual minaret on the southeast is only two storeys high. Three domes, elaborately ornamented with Multani tile work, surmount the mosque and library. In the profuse ornamentation of both the interior and exterior of the mosque with tile and mirror work, gilding, painting and calligraphy, the craftsmen have excelled in the use of a variety of materials – ivory, onyx, mother-of-pearl and even industrial tiles. The decorative motifs used are equally extravagant, being largely Mughal and Multani but also colonial. The Bhong Mosque reflects the flamboyant visual culture of the region, where trucks and rickshaws, books and clothes display a brilliance in colour and design.

MOSQUE OF HASSAN II, CASABLANCA, MOROCCO

When it was finally completed in 1993 after eight years of building, the Mosque of Hassan II was the largest mosque in the world, with an internal holding capacity of twenty-five thousand people, and eighty thousand if the outdoor esplanade area were to be used as an extension to the prayer hall.

Through the building of this monumental mosque, the Moroccan ruler, King Hassan II, who became monarch in 1961, was keen to establish his legitimacy as a descendant of the Prophet and thus a guardian of the faith. Also a patron of the arts, he wished to honour the rich architectural heritage of Morocco. Though the capital was in Rabat, the important commercial centre of Casablanca was in need of an icon to emphasize

Towering over the city of Casablanca, the minaret and mosque of King Hassan II makes a powerful statement of the imperial status of its patron. *Facing page:* Adapting vernacular forms in a contemporary idiom, the mosque of New Gourna is an attempt to revitalize the traditional earth technology of the area.

its importance for the state. The city was located on the coast and the mosque could therefore serve as a visual beacon, proclaiming the presence of Islam. Its monumental minaret aptly serves this function, and though it dwarfs the mass of the building, it is matched by the immensity of scale (the esplanade itself is 323,000 square feet [30,000 square metres]) of the complex.

Designed by architect Michel Pinseau, the complex includes hamams, conference and VIP rooms, a madrassa, a public library and museum, and the vast open esplanade. There is also underground parking for up to eleven hundred vehicles. The mosque was funded by about 13 million people.

Among its significant features, the square tower minaret rises to a height of 650 feet (200 metres), and like a lighthouse, throws out a laser beam up to 30 kilometres in the direction of Mecca. Part of the prayer hall can be rolled back to form an internal courtyard. This is possible due to the lightness of its roof tiles, which copy in aluminium the clay tiles of the Qarawiyin Mosque in Fez. Almost like a luxury resort, the ablutions chambers below the prayer hall have tiled lotus-blossom basins and fountains, hamams and a heated swimming pool.

VILLAGE MOSQUE, NEW GOURNA, EGYPT

This simple structure was conceived and built between 1945–48 with low-cost technology in mud brick and baked brick in a little village of seven thousand people near Luxor, an important site of ancient Egyptian tombs. The idea was to move the inhabitants away from the archaeological site, where they had been indulging in tomb robbing and destruction of ancient artifacts. The project was undertaken by the Egyptian Department of Antiquities. Hasan Fathy was the architect, a man renowned for his vision of alternate building technology.

Fathy's plan envisioned a completely new community environment where the mosque would be at the centre of other facilities such as housing, dispensary and women's social centre, primary schools for boys and girls, a market place, police station, village hall, theatre, sporting club, crafts exhibition hall and a Coptic church. At the time it was planned, Old Gourna's inhabitants were divided into four distinct tribes and accommodated in four distinct spaces around the central square and mosque.

The mosque is designed in the old Nubian style. Its form is defined by vaults, shallow domes and arched openings, devoid of any ornamentation. A vaulted gallery to the left of the southern entrance provides a resting place for passers-by

and visitors. In the centre is a courtyard and to its right the prayer hall, which is covered by a large dome with simple arched openings, and has small square bays with square columns supporting shallow domes. The ablutions area lies near the northern entrance. A staircase leads to the minaret.

As the need grew for other uses, such as a store room, guest area and study for the imam, the mosque grew in an organic manner, resulting in the irregular dimensions of these additional rooms. Lighting was an important consideration, as explained by Fathy himself in his book *Architecture for the Poor*: "To make a building that should have that sober and calm air that leads to quiet meditation and prayer, I had to consider how the light would fall upon its walls and be distributed in its rooms." Fathy's design has had a lasting influence on low-cost rural initiatives in the developing world.

CORNICHE MOSQUE, JEDDAH, SAUDI ARABIA

The smallest of three seafront mosques built in Jeddah, the Corniche Mosque was built in 1986 on an area of only 2,100 square feet (195 square metres). Located at the northern end of the corniche, which consists of reclaimed land, the mosque was part of a programme to beautify this popular recreational area. The architect El-Wakil suggested that a series of small mosques be built at regular intervals, which could serve as places of worship as well as act as large sculptural breaks between parks, restaurants and other decorative displays.

This compact building is composed of a small domed prayer hall with an antechamber covered by a barrel vault, an open court, a portico and a minaret. In the traditional style of the region, an external staircase leads to the minaret – an octagonal tower with an open balcony and a pointed cupola. Finials on the cupola and the main dome establish a visual connection between the main building and the minaret. The mosque is built of terracotta brick, plastered in white. Its concept is derived from the whitewashed buildings of the Mediterranean region and also by the vernacular idiom of Egypt.

The entrance is from the qibla side through the antechamber, leading to the inner court and prayer hall, where visitors have to make a complete turnaround to face the

Compact and elegant, the pristine white Corniche Mosque was built as part of a larger plan to beautify the seafront of Jeddah.
Facing page: **Vernacular Hausa architecture finds its place in the modern age in the Yaama Mosque, where mud brick, rammed earth and wood were used to create forms familiar to the community.**

unadorned mihrab niche. Although it incorporates all the traditional elements of the mosque, the recognizable historic imagery of the Corniche Mosque has been ingeniously interpreted in a contemporary vocabulary.

YAAMA MOSQUE, TAHOUA, NIGER

Designed by Falke Barmou, the builder-mason of the village, and funded entirely by members of the community, the Yaama Mosque is another example of a rural development initiative that respects traditional architecture. The decision to build a new Friday mosque in the Tahoua region of Niger was taken by the village elders in 1962. The building reached its final form in 1982. The original idea was of a simple rectangular hypostyle hall for prayer, with no additional functional spaces, not even a separate area for women. Even the required ablutions were to be carried out with the aid of a water jar kept in a corner of the site.

In the course of time, the additions that have been made have been purely ornamental, though they have radically changed the image of the building. The original area was only 3,230 square feet (300 square metres), with five rows of columns in it. Mud brick and rammed earth construction of the region necessitated the use of thick columns, closely spaced, and thick load-bearing walls to support the roof, which was formed of criss-crossed beams made of bundles of sticks, filled in and covered with mud. This technique could not prevent the roof from leaking, however, and it was later replaced by arched supports also made with bundles of sticks. These were supported by mud and straw mortar voussoirs. At this time, a dome was built over the central part of the prayer hall.

This traditional Hausa method of mud construction requires continual renewal after the rains. These periods were taken advantage of to make the changes. In 1978, the floor area was almost doubled, with the additional construction of four corner towers.

REGENT'S PARK MOSQUE, LONDON

When it was built in 1977 there were about thirty-five mosques in Great Britain and almost four hundred public places of prayer to serve the needs of half a million Muslims living in the country. The site was chosen on the suggestion of the Egyptian ambassador in 1940 that the British government allocate a plot of land for a mosque as a reciprocal arrangement for the Egyptians having done the same in Cairo for the building of an Anglican church.

The mosque is one of several such international projects that came into being in the 1950s as more and more Islamic

community signifies its growing importance as a minority group in England.

The design, by Sir Frederick Gibberd, has three components to the plan. These include the mosque, an Islamic cultural centre and living accommodation for the staff. Gibberd's design, which combines all three into one unified composition, underlines, in his words, that "Islam is not just a religious observance but a way of life." When required, the rectangular prayer hall can be extended laterally on to terraces covered by canopies through a system of folding doors. From a capacity of 965 worshippers in the prayer hall, the mosque can accommodate 4,500 people through the use of extended areas.

The most important element, the qibla wall, overlooks Regent's Park and faces Mecca. Only the minaret and golden dome predominate the surroundings because of their height, without overshadowing other historic buildings, while the local Derbyshire stone is used as the building material so that the mosque can merge with the built environment around it.

As in London, Islamic cultural centres incorporating mosques have been built in other metropolitan cities of the world. They serve as focal points for meetings, research activities, discourses, and other cultural or charitable activities for rapidly expanding Muslim communities. They respond to the increasingly sophisticated needs of the believer today – to nourish both the intellect and the spirit.

KING FAISAL MOSQUE, ISLAMABAD, PAKISTAN

nations proclaimed their independent status and wished to establish their identity in non-Muslim countries. The centrally located site selected by the British Muslim

In sharp contrast to traditional Mughal architecture in Pakistan is the King Faisal Mosque in Islamabad, named after its benefactor, the monarch of Saudi Arabia. Symbol of the

The site for the Regent's Park Mosque in London was given to the Muslim community as early as 1944 but it was only after an international competition in 1969 that the design was selected. *Facing page:* The sheer size and exterior boldness of King Faisal's Mosque is matched by the awesome spaces inside and the striking sculptural and decorative composition of its minbar and qibla.

new capital city of Pakistan, its four rocket-like minarets at the corners reach upwards, towards heaven as it were, and represent the emerging status of a vibrant new nation.

The mosque was designed in 1968 by a Turkish architect, to accommodate a hundred thousand people. Vedat Dalokay, who won the commission through an international competition open only to Muslim architects, proposed a tent-like structure, this shape being "behind any large single-vaulted space. I would describe the mosque," he said, "as the last tent of the Margalla hills, an extension of the hills – on the plains." Situated at the northern end of Islamabad, a destination rather than a focal point of the city, the mosque's main point of reference is the Margalla hills, a captivating backdrop to a strikingly imaginative structure.

Apart from the hundred thousand worshippers in the designated spaces of the mosque, including a women's prayer gallery for fifteen hundred directly above the main entrance, the open-air areas alone can accommodate two hundred thousand. The complex incorporates the Islamic Research Institute offices and the International Islamic University but these are independent of the main prayer hall.

Insistence on modern materials rather than readily available brick and stone allowed for the latest structural technology, which facilitated a space-frame structure of triangular folded concrete plates meeting at the centre. In between each plate, tapering glazed slits provide natural light to the prayer hall. The strikingly modern interior is overwhelming in its vertical scale, with the qibla wall decorated with blue and gold mosaic Iznik tiles depicting Islamic calligraphy.

The mosque has consciously eschewed all references to

Muslim architecture of the region, perhaps in its bid to proclaim the birth of a new nation freeing itself from the hold of other regionally contextual forms. Only the minarets, however, with their triangular, pointed tips, are obviously inspired by Ottoman architecture in a gesture of acceptance of the contribution of the largest, most robust and most victorious of Muslim empires.

From its earliest days when the jami (congregational, or Friday) mosque was closely associated with political authority, the mosque has several incarnations today. In modern times, while the state or community or individual may be the source from which a mosque derives its power or visual imagery, it still remains, as in history, the symbol of a collective identity, adapting in form or fashion but always retaining the basic elements that typified the very first places of Muslim congregational worship.

The Badshahi Mosque, Pakistan.
Following page 144: Berber women in Grand
Atlas Mountains, Morocco.

Glossary

Bay: Transversal spatial unit in a covered space.

Caliph: Head of the Islamic community in the line of the Prophet's successors.

Chajja: Protective overhang over wall opening.

Hamam: Public or private baths like the Roman baths.

Haram: Consecrated space in a mosque for rituals and prayer.

Horseshoe arch: A three-quarter arch on a rectangular wall opening.

Hypostyle hall: A hall or other large space with a roof supported by columns or pillars forming multiple naves and bays.

Imam: Arabic term meaning the leader of ritual prayer. For Shiites, the imam is the head of the religious community.

Iwan: Vaulted architectural space with façade mostly opening towards a courtyard.

Jaali: Perforated ornamental screen.

Liwan: The pillared and roofed main sanctuary of a mosque.

Madrassa: Koranic school whose architecutral form follows the tradtition of mosques.

Mahdi: Shias believe him to be the hidden imam who would reappear at the end of time.

Maqsura: Enclosure around the most sacred area of the mosque, where the sovereign attended prayers.

Merlon: Part of parapet between wall openings.

Mihrab: The central arched niche in the rear wall of a mosque.

Minbar: Raised seat or pulpit to the right of the mihrab.

Muqarnas: Graduated division of arch corners into miniature niches; also ornamental stalactites placed in tiers resembling a honeycomb adorning corners, cupolas, entrance portals and decorative surfaces

Nave: Longitudinal area in a covered building, as opposed to the transversal bay.

Pendentive: Curved triangle linking structure to the dome.

Pishtaq: Persian term for large screen framing an iwan.

Qibla: Wall of the mosque oriented to the direction of Mecca, in which the mihrab is placed.

Ribat: Monastic fort.

Seraglio: A sultan's palace.

Temenos: Greek term meaning a sacred space or precinct.

Transept: Main aisle cutting across smaller aisles.

Voussoirs: Wedge-shaped stones forming the structure of an arch on either side of the keystone.

Ziyada: Outer courtyard surrounding a mosque, separating it from its urban surroundings.

Bibliography

Amin, Mohd, Duncan Willetts, Bendan Farrow, *Pakistan, From Mountains to Sea*. Camerapin Publishers International, Nairobi, 1994.

Bloom, Jonathan and Sheila Blair, *Islamic Arts*. Phaidon Press Ltd, London, 1997.

Central Asia, Gems of 9th-19th Century Architecture. Planeta Publishers, 1987.

Davies, Philip, *The Penguin Guide to the Monuments of India. Vol II: Islamic, Rajput, European*. Penguin Books, London, 1989.

Ertug, Ahmed, *Istanbul: City of Domes*. Ahmed Ertug, Istanbul, 1992.

Grover, Satish, *Islamic Architecture in India*. 2nd ed, CBS Publishers & Distributors, New Delhi, 2002.

Hattstein, Markus and Delius, Peter (eds.), *Islam: Art and Architecture*, Konemann, 2000.

Hoag, John D, *Western Islamic Architecture*. Studio Vista Ltd, London, 1968.

Holod, Renata and Hasan-Uddin Khan, *The Mosque and the Modern World*. Thames and Hudson Ltd, London, 1997.

Kidwai, Azra, *Islam*. Roli Books Pvt. Ltd., Lustre Press, 1998.

Nuttgens, Patrick, *The Story of Architecture*. Phaidon Press Ltd, London, 1983.

Stierlin, Henri, *Islam. Early Architecture. Vol 1: From Baghdad to Cordoba*. Taschen Verlag, Cologne, 1996.

Stierlin, Henri, *Turkey, From the Seljuks to the Ottomans*. Taschen Verlag, Cologne, 1998.